Leadology

12 Ideas To *Level Up* Your Leadership

I0154118

Written By

John**Barrett**

Published By
Rocket Publishing

Leadology

12 Ideas To *Level Up* Your Leadership

John **Barrett**

Published By: Rocket Publishing

Book Design By: John Barrett Art

www.johnbarrettart.com

ISBN-10: 0-9888284-4-8

ISBN-13: 978-0-9888284-4-5

Table Of Contents

Vision is the lens that keeps an organization in focus. Without vision, there is no clarity. If leaders don't know where they are going, they won't inspire others to take the journey with them

Growth is not an automatic process. We do not magically get better. We only get better when we are planted in the right environment.

Leaders are always finding creative ways to accelerate their team's progress. The more a leader can do to generate momentum, the further the team will go.

The most important person you will ever lead is yourself. Leadership is more about who you are than what you do.

Teamwork multiplies your effort. One can accomplish much, but two can accomplish much more. Building a great team will determine how far your impact will go.

The higher you go, the more pressure there is to perform. Always ascending and never stabilizing eventually causes burnout. Leaders must practice the art of balancing the stress of success and the renewal of rest.

Special Thanks To…

My mentor, Dr. John C Maxwell, for pouring wisdom, encouragement, and direction into my leadership journey.

My parents, for being the greatest examples of leadership I have ever observed.

My wife and kids, for teaching me the best leadership principles in the classroom of life.

The Next-Level Leader

With every step, great leaders advance their leadership ability to the next level. They never stop challenging themselves to reach new heights. They know the secret to success is the capacity to lead themselves and others effectively. In fact, true success is simply an overflow of great leadership. But so many leaders and organizations feel frustratingly stuck without any hope of making it to the summit of their dreams. As a result, they question if they have what it takes to get to that next level. Constant doubt leads to continual insecurity.

Instead of fighting to move forward, they fight to maintain. Instead of breaking through, they break down in defeat. Their solution? Work harder. But in doing so, they're just spinning their wheels in the mud without catching any traction. With so much demanding their attention, they have no margin for what they should be doing. They're so caught up in the present they have no capacity to accelerate forward. Because of this tension, leaders all over the world have begun to run out of emotional gas. They have great ideas, but no time or energy to implement them.

It's not passion they necessarily lack, but precision on how to make it happen. They are left wondering how to break out of the rut.

This is part of why I wrote *Leadology*.

This book is designed to skyrocket your leadership to the next level. You will get ideas that are going to help you get unstuck as you discover what it takes to be a great leader. By leveling up you *can* become the leader you are capable of being. Success doesn't come from the luck of the draw, happenstance, or being in the right place at the right time. Success is the strategic, intentional effort of always looking up rather than always looking down.

When asked about his country's greatest weapon against the Nazi regime, Winston Churchill didn't hesitate to reply, "It was what England's greatest weapon had always been...hope." What Churchill knew, and what all great leaders know, is that a leader's most empowering "weapon" is hope. It is unquestionably the strongest motivational force you can use. When hope fills the heart, dreams of a better future overflow into reality. Hope makes the seemingly impossible become possible. We begin to see opportunities that otherwise would have remained hidden. Capitalism itself is built on the premise of hope; the hope that your effort will bring you success.

The bravery of all exploration derives from the probability of more. One will never step out into uncharted territory without the hope that they can get to somewhere better. Next-level leaders are hope-driven people who are always advancing upward. They stay above the fray by moving their focus from what *is* to what *can be*. When you level up your leadership capacity, you level up everyone and everything around you. President John F. Kennedy once said, "A rising tide lifts all boats." Great leaders are not just a big boat; they are the rising tide itself.

The 12 ideas in this book will bring your leadership performance to a higher level. Oliver Wendell Holmes said, "One's mind, once stretched by a new idea, never regains its original dimensions." As you journey through *Leadology*, your mind will stretch with examples, tips, and strategies to empower your leadership ability. When you are filled with the content from this book, your cognitive awareness will become a leadership library archive. You will then be able to access this library in any given situation and know how to lead through it. As your cognitive leadership library increases, it catapults your ability to lead effectively.

> "As your cognitive leadership library increases, it catapults your ability to lead effectively."

This is why leaders are readers; they constantly fill their minds with quotes, stories, experiences, stats, and ideas to level up. Great leadership starts with information, and this information leads to transformation. The transformation begins in them first and then transforms the world around them. If you study the most highly successful people throughout history, a common trait you will find in them is an insatiable obsession with knowledge. It is not surprising that we find them studying their craft at a minimum of an hour a day, if not tremendously more.

Because of this, Speaker Earl Nightingale taught us that to become an expert in any given field, you must spend one hour a day, every day, for five years studying it. Or, as modern day author and psychologist Malcom Gladwell calls it, "The 10,000 Hour Rule." We cannot improve that which we are unaware of. So to improve, we must first open ourselves up to resources that will ignite our capacity to learn. It is through information that we open the door to transformation.

I have found that when you level up your leadership, you will transform at least four vital components in your life:

1) Your Ideas

You are only one idea away from a major breakthrough. A simple thought can become the catalyst for a life-altering future. When you open up your mind to new ideas, you open up to new opportunities. All it takes is one idea to catapult you from where you are to where you want to be. Inspiration is the pathway to innovation. The more you level up your leadership ability, the more you'll create better practices, better strategies, and better opportunities. Author John Steinbeck said, "Ideas are like rabbits. You get a couple and learn how to handle them, and pretty soon you have a dozen." Here is the definition of the verb *Inspire*: to encourage somebody to greater effort, enthusiasm, or

> "Inspiration is the pathway to innovation."

creativity: to awaken a particular feeling in somebody. [Latin-*inspirare* "to breathe."] When you take the time to develop yourself, you'll awaken the leader within.

2) Your Influence

Influence is the currency of leadership. To lead others, you must influence them. John Quincy Adams said, "If your actions inspire others to dream more, learn more, do more, and become more, you are a leader." People do not follow people they disrespect. Having a title doesn't make you a leader; having influence is what makes you a leader. When you level up your leadership ability, your influence allows you to be, do, and have more. The more influence you gain, the more you are able to accomplish.

> "Most people are busy trying to accumulate 'stuff,' but if you want to make a mark, then invest your life into accumulating influence."

Most people are busy trying to accumulate "stuff," but if you want to make a mark, then invest your life into accumulating influence.

3) Your Impact

Your positive impact is one of the most valuable treasures you can leave behind on this Earth. It is your biggest footprint. It outdoes your financial status, fame, and all the material possessions you could ever acquire. Legacy is a gift that can change people's destiny. We have all been impacted by friends and family members that have passed on before us, and when we take a look at their lives, hopefully, we are effected by who they were and the positive impact they were able to make. Author Shannon L. Alder said, "Carve your name on hearts, not tombstones. A legacy is etched into the minds of others and the stories they share about you."

What kind of impact will you have when you have passed on? What will others say about the legacy you left behind? What will you be remembered for? How will you be remembered? Our legacy starts now—not when we are gone. This is good news. This means we get to choose what kind of legacy we will pass on. When you level up your leadership ability, you create a greater impact from your life, and that is worth more than anything.

4) Your Income

When your leadership goes to the next level you'll raise your value to the company and to those around you. Great leaders receive greater compensation because of what they bring to the table. In 1921, Charles Schwab was one of the first American businessmen to be paid over a million-dollar salary by U.S. Steel owner Andrew Carnegie. What's interesting is that Schwab didn't know much at all about steel or manufacturing. In fact, he let it be known that his workers knew much more than he about the business. But this is what Schwab said about why he was paid so well: "I consider my ability to arouse enthusiasm among my people the greatest asset I possess, and the way to develop the best that is in a person is by appreciation and encouragement." Schwab became incredibly wealthy by becoming a great leader.

Is it all about the money? Of course not. But as Zig Ziglar always said, "Money won't make you happy, but everybody wants to find out for themselves." The truth is, creating wealth only opens up the door for more opportunities to provide for yourself, your family, your charities, and the impact you want to make. As you level up your leadership ability you'll level up your capacity to make more money. Leadership learners are exceptional earners.

You are about to unleash the next-level leader within you as you dive into all the ideas in *Leadology*. There is no chronological or systematic order to this book. Each idea stands alone as a means to inspire you to grow in your leadership. At the end of

> "Reflective thinking opens the door for future possibilities."

each idea, there are a series of questions to help engage you in the leveling-up process. Please take the time to use the questions as a tool to empower yourself with self-reflective insight. Reflective thinking opens the door for future possibilities. Socrates observed, "The unexamined life is not worth living." Your answers to the questions in this book will enable you to understand what you've done, what you are currently doing, and what you should be doing. I encourage you to read one idea a week for the next 12 weeks, and then apply the principles you have learned.

Take your team through this book as well. You can use one idea a week or month to evaluate your leadership within the context of each topic. Read through the challenges and use the questions as kick-starters for discussion. By doing this, you will finish the book in 12 weeks, allowing time for you and your team to cover a broad stroke of talking points. It will unify your teammates, creating a cohesive context of leading at the next level. Teams that grow together win together.

May you level up your leadership as you journey through the 12 ideas in *Leadology*...enjoy!

THE

EYE
Exam

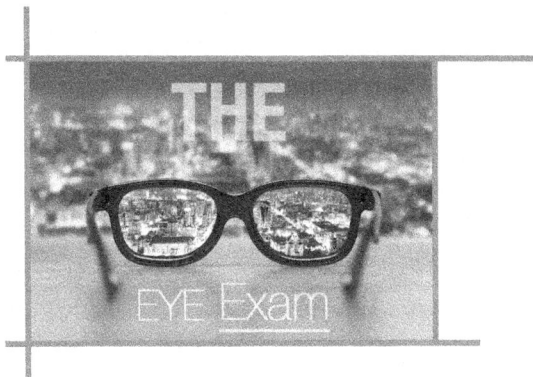

The Eye Exam

Vision is the lens that keeps an organization in focus. Without vision, there is no clarity. If leaders don't know where they are going, they won't inspire others to take the journey with them. It is not that vision is powerful in and of itself; it is its effect on people that makes it an irresistible force.

Years ago, I noticed that my eyes were becoming a little blurry. I didn't think I needed glasses. But after much coaxing, my wife convinced me to finally get an eye exam. The local optometrist ran me through the usual tests and determined that I did, in fact, need glasses. I still wasn't convinced.

That's what they always say, right?

I knew my eyes were not in bad shape. But what was I going to do? It was me against a professional...and my wife. I reluctantly picked out some frames and ordered my new glasses. After a few days I got the call that my order was in. I will never forget what happened when I picked up my new glasses. The optometrist's assistant wanted me to "test out" my new prescription before I left. I was ready to get this over with, go home, and place the glasses in a drawer somewhere to gather dust.

But I complied with the secretary's wishes, put them on, and...I gasped at what I saw. Objects had edges instead of blurs! There were colors around me that I had forgotten even existed. Things went from standard definition to high-def. instantly, and I was simply elated. I couldn't wait to see what the rest of the world looked like.

I dashed out of the office and was immediately amazed when I looked at the trees surrounding me. My memories from childhood were true. Trees really did have leaves and not just little green blobs hanging from each branch. My wife was waiting for me in the car, clearly taken aback by my odd behavior. I had to tell her what I was seeing. I opened the car door and WOW! Who was this beauty sitting next to me? I mean, I knew she was pretty, but WOW! I spent the whole drive home taking in everything I saw with awe and wonder.

Glasses give me the clarity I need in order to see things as they truly are. In the same way, vision helps your team come into complete focus. You must be able to give them a clear depiction of your target. When a leader paints a sure picture of *why* they are doing what they are doing and *where* they are going, a team can harmonize with one another and with the organization. The clearer the vision, the more productive people will be.

Christopher Wren, one of the greatest architects in London, was commissioned to build Saint Paul's Cathedral after the great fire of 1666. While observing three bricklayers working on a scaffold, Wren asked, "What are you doing?"

The first man who was crouched replied, "Just making a living."

The second man who was halfway standing said, "Just building a wall."

The third man who was working hard and determined said, "Creating a cathedral for the Almighty."

Indeed, the last man knew what his true work was all about; his vision was clear.

When your team knows what they are working toward, they will be better equipped to make it happen. But if your team is unclear about the vision, they will not know how to properly use their time and energy. Zig Ziglar said, "If you aim at nothing you will hit it every time." Or to put it another way, Proverbs 29:18 tells us, "Where there is no vision, the people perish." A leader must be the one to keep the vision alive by making it visible in all that they do.

Unfortunately, vision blurs over time. We begin to naturally lose enthusiasm. People need to be continually reminded about why they are doing what they are doing. Government official Paul Nitze said, "One of the most dangerous forms of human error is forgetting what one is trying to achieve."

A vision will push someone to work with a stronger sense of dedication and purpose. One of our greatest presidents, Ronald Reagan, used to say, "Our best days are ahead of us." President Reagan knew how to keep the eyes of the country looking forward to a better future. In a time when the American people worried deeply about inflation, economic decline, the Cold War, drug abuse, and a host of other challenges, Reagan focused on what *could be*. He boldly changed the landscape of the country, and it started with his optimistic vision: The Shining City on a Hill. When there is a sense of hope for the future, there is a surge of power in the present.

Imagine how many employees know their company's vision. The statistics would shock you. Most vision statements are institutionalized within a poster on the wall rather than internalized within the hearts of the people. A leader's job is to make sure they genuinely weave in the vision and values of the organization as often and best as they can. Many times a team only hears about the vision and values of their organization in a conference meeting at the beginning of the year, and then never hears about it again until next year's meeting. The managers then wonder where the low morale is coming from.

When it comes to vision and values, leaders have to display it, say it, spray it, wheel it, deal it, and seal it. You have to help the vision stick in the hearts of the people with clarity, conviction, confidence, and commitment.

Let's break these down.

> "When it comes to vision and values, leaders have to display it, say it, spray it, wheel it, deal it, and seal it."

1) Clarity

When the Green Bay Packers football team hired Vince Lombardi as their new coach, he was committed to the challenge of turning the franchise around. He began leading practices, inspiring, training, and motivating everyone on the team. But at one point in a particular practice, he became so frustrated with the players' performance that he finally blew the whistle.

"Everybody stop and gather around," he said. Then he knelt down, picked up the pigskin, and said, "Let's start at the beginning. This is a football. These are the yard markers. I'm the coach. You are the players." He went on, in the most elementary of ways, to explain the basic fundamentals of football. Coach Lombardi brought back focus to what the team needed to remember. It's the clarity of a vision that unifies the team. When tasks get foggy and vague, confusion begins to set in. Unclear expectations produce unmet results.

Three ingredients will generate clarity: simplicity, brevity, and specificity.

Keep It Simple

Aeronautical engineer Clarence "Kelly" Johnson created a famous acronym while working on complicated design protocols in the 1960s. He implemented the KISS principle: Keep It Simple Stupid. The saying helped his team remember that systems work best when kept uncomplicated. Simplicity is always the best course of action. It is the process of eliminating everything that is unnecessary. Complicated procedures and red tape only create frustration and limited participation. Resist the urge to create more rules and regulations. Complexity breeds confusion, confusion breeds chaos, chaos breeds contempt, and contempt breeds *carelessness*. When a leader makes things difficult, they make things worse. You should always minimize steps to the simplest form without losing excellence. Journalist C. W. Ceran said, "Genius is the ability to reduce the complicated to the simple."

Keep It Short

My daughters love to play telephone with their friends. One starts out with a phrase and whispers it in a friend's ear. Then she will whisper the phrase, to the best of her ability, in her friend's ear. This goes on until the last person has to say the phrase out loud. I have never heard the original phrase correctly stated at the end of the round. In fact, the larger the group, the more distorted the message gets. In the same way, the larger your organization grows, the greater the need for simplicity and clarity. Keeping things easily memorable accomplishes clarity. The longer it takes to explain the vision, the more room there is for confusion. Albert Einstein put it this way: "If you can't explain it to a six-year-old, you don't understand it yourself." Every organization should have specific words and phrases that are easily internalized and that genuinely communicate the vision. These words and phrases assist in keeping the vision alive. The vision must be portable, repeatable, and shareable by everyone.

Keep It Specific

As organizations grow, they are tempted to keep adding to their mission and vision. A company always needs to be growing and expanding, but should not add so much that it loses its identity. The enticement to be a smorgasbord catch-all rather than a specialized service can be the downfall of success. Many companies lose sight of their original mission and purpose when they start to become generalized rather than specific. It takes intentional effort to stay true to your vision when everyone and everything will call you to keep doing more. Starbucks faced this issue years ago. The company felt they were getting away from their original vision that made them successful in the first place. CEO Howard Shultz addressed getting back to who they intended to be in a letter he sent out to his stores in 2007. Here is a snippet:

> *"I take full responsibility myself, but we desperately need to look into the mirror and realize it's time to get back to the core and make the changes necessary to evoke the heritage, the tradition, and the passion that we all have for the true Starbucks experience."*

Starbucks continued to lead the way in coffee shop innovation and it remains so with a clear vision.

2) Conviction

One of the defining traits of great leaders is a deep conviction in their cause. They exude a passion forged by the belief that what they are doing truly matters. You will never meet a highly effective leader who does not have a strong burden for their cause. A leader without conviction will never accomplish their mission. There are too many obstacles that will derail them along the way. However, when a leader has conviction, they are able to inspire others to believe in the cause. People are willing to significantly invest into those

> "Teams fueled by a worthy cause stay the course even when the going gets tough."

who believe in what they do. Teams fueled by a worthy cause stay the course even when the going gets tough.

An aid group in South Africa sent a message to missionary and explorer David Livingston. It said, "Have you found a good road to where you are?" To this, Livingston replied, "If you have men who will only come if they know there is a good road, I don't want them. I want men who will come even if there is no road at all." Livingston knew how important it was for his team to be people of deep conviction; otherwise they would have abandoned the mission at the first sign of resistance.

What pushes a soldier out of the bunker and into the line of fire? A cause. What drives an athlete to train for years for an Olympic opportunity that may only last minutes? A cause. What makes a firefighter run into a burning building and risk their life? A cause. Never underestimate the power of a cause. Without it, there is no incentive to act, no incentive to sacrifice, no incentive to practice. But with it comes a motivation that pushes us beyond what we thought possible. British Prime Minister Benjamin Disraeli said, "I have brought myself, by long meditation, to the conviction that a human being with a settled purpose must accomplish it, and that nothing can resist a will which will stake even existence upon its fulfillment." One of the toughest responsibilities leadership requires is the assignment to inspire others to a worthy cause. The significance of a vision will determine the sacrifice people are willing to make for it.

3) Confidence

Abraham Lincoln said, "The probability that we may fail in the struggle ought not to deter us from the support of a cause we believe to be just." Lincoln's confidence in doing what was right was more important than doing what was popular. Lincoln was a man of confidence—not so much in himself, but in his cause. He was so confident in his cause that he would speak boldly about slavery even in hostile environments. He once made a bold challenge, saying, "Whenever I hear anyone arguing for slavery, I feel a strong impulse to see it tried on him personally."

Having confidence in your cause is not based on calculating the odds; it is based on being courageous enough to do what needs to be done. Many people feel they need to know every detail to be confident in a task, but confidence is more than knowledge. It is about believing in your ability to make things work. It is the trust that you will keep moving forward, even when you're *not* sure what lies ahead. Confidence allows us to break through our limits and expand our borders. If we only move forward in the things we know, we will never explore greater opportunities. Limiting ourselves to only act on what we are comfortable with will only get us what we've always got. We must be willing to step out in confidence and break the barrier of comfort. T.S. Elliot said, "Only those who will risk going too far can possibly find out how far one can go."

The comfort zone consists of only what we have experienced. We know what we are capable of in this zone, but to expand our opportunities we have to expand our boundaries. Everyone and every organization have "comfort zones." These zones are the mental spaces that people operate within. They are artificial boundaries to make them feel a sense of emotional security in their work and decision-making. What distinguishes leaders from followers is what they do with their "comfort zones." There are those who are perfectly happy staying warm and cozy in this safe box they've built, and then there are those who constantly push and test the limits of their abilities. Those who test the limits are those who achieve greatness. The difference between successful people and unsuccessful people lies not in what they know, but in what they are willing to do.

> "The difference between successful people and unsuccessful people lies not in what they know, but in what they are willing to do."

All growth takes place outside of our perceived limits. Author Neale Donald Walsch said, "Life begins at the end of your comfort zone." You will never reach your potential by only doing what you are comfortable doing as a leader, and your team will never reach their potential by only doing what they are comfortable doing. You will have to venture out into areas you know nothing about in order to eventually know something about it. It takes action to get a result. You cannot get better in the things you have never done unless you do them. To improve a result, you first have to get a result. Never allow others to be governed by indecision and procrastination, for they will get stuck in the paralysis of analysis. Be confident in the vision as you keep stretching people to push it forward.

To grow, you have to step out of the comfort zone and into the confidence zone.

4) Commitment

On May 29, 1953, Sir Edmund Hillary and Nepalese Sherpa mountaineer, Tenzing Norgay, became the first men in history to climb Mt. Everest. They traveled through extreme conditions in brutally freezing temperatures, but only because they were committed to this life-threatening task. Many had tried to reach the summit before but had given up just short of the goal. Sir Hillary once said, "If you cannot understand that there is something in man which responds to the challenge of this mountain and goes out to meet it, that the struggle is the struggle of life itself upward and forever upward, then you won't see why we go."

Mountain climbers such as Sir Hillary and Norgay could never scale a significant mountain without an unwavering sense of commitment to the journey. In the same way, we cannot get to the mountaintop of success without the same kind of commitment and determination to the vision. Only climbing when we "feel like it" will never take us to new heights. We only get to the top by hard work and endurance. "Feeling like it" may get you started, but it won't keep you going. When faced with obstacles and challenges, many people surrender. But to reach the top, you will always have to fight through the setbacks and unforeseen challenges. Remember this: You cannot climb a smooth mountain. It is the rocky places that we can use to become better and stronger. If we only travel the familiar paths we will never find the hidden treasures. Ken Blanchard says, "There's a difference between interest and commitment. When you are interested in doing something, you do it only when it is convenient. When you are committed to something, you accept no excuses."

> "If we only travel the familiar paths we will never find the hidden treasures."

Many obstacles will test a leader's resolve to keep their attention on the vision. We face challenges every day that can easily jolt our focus off what truly matters. Daniel Boone explored the great wilderness of Tennessee and Kentucky. It was Boone who marked the Wilderness Road that brought settlers into the new land. He often wandered over vast areas of forest, living off the land and dodging arrows. Even though he navigated uncharted territory, he kept on his mission to become familiar with the land. Asked if he had ever been lost, he replied, "No…but I was a mite confused once for about three or four days, though!" Boone knew how to stay positive.

Leaders have to be the ones who stay on target, even when things get shaky. They have to become the anchor in the storm for their team. When everyone else begins to panic and allow negative thinking to consume them, leaders have to be the ones displaying genuine optimism. Gilbert Arland said, "When an archer misses the mark, he turns and looks for the fault within himself. Failure to hit the bull's-eye is never the fault of the target. To improve your aim—improve yourself."

Keep your team's eyes on the objectives, not the obstacles. If leaders expect their followers to commit themselves to the vision, then those leaders must demonstrate their own high commitment to the vision. Leaders accomplish this through a focused personal dedication to stay on target and keep their eyes forward. A leader must keep aimed at the vision each and every day while displaying hope to those around them. Former IBM Chairman and CEO Thomas J. Watson said, "Nothing so conclusively proves a man's ability to lead others, as what he does from day to day to lead himself."

Questions To Think About:

A) Define the vision of your organization in a few sentences.

_____

_____

_____

B) On a scale from 1-10 (10 being the strongest) individually rate how strong the four C's (Clarity, Conviction, Confidence, Commitment) are in your team.

Clarity   1 2 3 4 5 6 7 8 9 10

Conviction   1 2 3 4 5 6 7 8 9 10

Confidence   1 2 3 4 5 6 7 8 9 10

Commitment   1 2 3 4 5 6 7 8 9 10

C) Write down one way you can you improve each one of the four C's in your organization?

Clarity

_____

Conviction

_____

Confidence

_____

Commitment

_____

Leadology Challenge:

For most organizations, it has been a while since they've reevaluated the vision and mission of their cause. Time passes, situations change, and opportunities redirect the overall direction. We should always be reevaluating along the journey of our mission. Like a heat-seeking missile that is constantly course-correcting to lock on its target, we need to always be correcting our propensity to drift off course. Jonas Salk, the man who developed the polio vaccine, said, "Life is an error-making and error-correcting process." I fully agree with that statement, and would add that leadership operates by the same principle.

Set up an extended meeting with your team to discuss the vision of your organization. Get realigned with the mission of your cause. Challenge yourself and your team to find any areas where you may be drifting off course. Also, dialogue about the areas that you have stayed the course and need to remain steady. Use this time as a "refresh button" to make sure everyone is on the same page. These types of meetings need to be proactive, not reactive. Many companies only refresh the vision when things are going wrong, but great companies are continuously reinforcing the vision by bringing everyone together to communicate around the cause before it gets off course.

The
BONSAI
TREE

|| Idea #2 ||

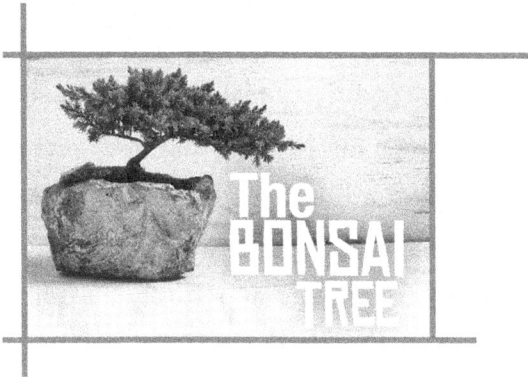

The Bonsai Tree

Growth is not an automatic process. We do not magically get better. We only get better when we are planted in the right environment. An organization grows to its potential when its people grow to their potential.

Growing up, my family and I went to the state fair every year. The summer humidity made it so hot as we walked for miles around the fairgrounds. I always looked forward to escaping the heat by visiting the air-conditioned Exposition Building. This was a huge warehouse full of hundreds of vendors selling every type of gadget and gizmo imaginable. I will never forget the year that we came across a booth selling Bonsai trees. These trees were fascinating, and since I was a die-hard fan of the movie *The Karate Kid*, I had always wanted to be like Daniel LaRusso, planting Bonsai trees with my very own Mr. Miagi. I figured this was my opportunity.

Somehow, I convinced my parents to purchase a tree for me and I carefully transported my prized possession home. I was now thoroughly convinced that I had been endowed with a mastery of the art of karate simply by becoming the proud owner of my very own Bonsai. Reality soon hit. I had no idea how hard it was going to be to take care of a Bonsai tree. Everyday I had to make sure the tree was in direct sunlight for a very specific amount of time; no more, no less. I also had to precisely measure its water intake. And to top it all off, I had to delicately trim my tree with a precision that only Mr. Miagi had mastered. This proved to be much more work than this twelve-year-old karate kid was willing to do. Besides, I needed more time to practice my kicks and punches; I didn't have time to perfect the art of gardening. You can imagine what happened over the course of a few weeks. Eventually the tree died, and with it, my dreams of becoming the next karate kid. You see, the tree couldn't survive without a proper growth environment. Unless it was nurtured and exposed to what it needed to grow, it didn't have a chance. If I had just kept the tree healthy, I might have been the martial arts master that I dreamed of being.

Just like my Bonsai tree needed sunlight to develop, your team needs exposure to growth opportunities to bloom. Cultivating a fertile growth environment is what separates successful companies from average ones. Every gardener knows you have to water what you want to grow. When you plant a tree in a small pot, it will stop growing once it reaches the walls of the pot. The tree is not the problem; it's the environment that is limiting growth. To grow the tree, you have to put it in an environment that will allow it to develop without borders. The more room there is for growth, the larger the tree can become. Likewise, people need the proper surroundings to fully develop into highly effective leaders. Author Napoleon Hill said, "We begin to see, therefore, the importance of selecting our environment with the greatest of care, because environment is the mental feeding ground out of which the food that goes into our minds is extracted."

Failing to create an environment where people are growing will slowly erode morale and stifle progress. As a leader, it is your responsibility to build a developmental greenhouse for your people to become everything they're capable of. When leaders water the seeds of potential in others, productivity increases. Your organization will only be as good as the people running it. If you want your organization to be great, you have to equip your people to be even greater.

> "If you want your organization to be great, you have to equip your people to be even greater."

Too many companies spend all of their time using internal procedures and rules of operations to orient people rather than developing them into self-thinking leaders. They expend exorbitant amounts of energy training people in job descriptions rather than mindsets. If your team isn't being developed to step out further, think out of the box, and learn new skills, they will be limited to stay exactly the same. Who they are now will be the person they'll remain, never growing to greater heights.

The lack of growth environments is a systemic issue that began when organizations started placing production over people. With the boom of the Industrial Revolution in the late 1700s into the 1800s, institutions started training children in a way to prepare them for routine factory work. Students were no longer challenged to be leaders with unique skill sets. They were trained to be cookie-cutter workers who follow orders, keep production up, and maintain the flow. Generations have since been conditioned to work like this. You'll see this type of supervising in the way many businesses are run today. Follow the manual, uphold the routines, do your job as it's written, and don't ask questions. There is not much emphasis on recognizing a person for who they are and developing the unique strengths that person brings to the table.

The organizations breaking away from this mentality are the ones seeing breakthroughs in innovation and achieving staggering results. They are refusing to be limited by the dogmas that have been imposed upon them. They are committed to developing their people to be thinkers, pioneers, and leaders. High-quality workers are being drawn to these organizations because of the engaging culture they provide. Benjamin Franklin said, "Without continual growth and progress, such words as improvement, achievement, and success have no meaning."

Creating a growth environment takes three areas of commitment:

1) Make Time To Grow

To increase someone's ability, you must intentionally develop them. The most successful companies don't just hire people; they develop people. Make sure your team is allotted enough time to grow into their leadership abilities. It's amazing to see that most organization's job descriptions say nothing about the responsibility of personal development. But these organizations fail to see that as the individual grows, so grows their abilities to add

> "The most successful companies don't just hire people; they develop people."

value to the organization. And because of this, personal and professional development must be one of the first points communicated in any job description. These times of growth need to be woven into the expectations of the workweek. Too many organizations assume their people will take time to grow outside of the office, but this rarely happens when left up to chance. Not only does the person suffer from a lack of developing himself or herself in this situation, but also the organization suffers an even greater loss. As the leader, you will need to encourage your people in their growth development. Make sure your team is utilizing intentional time to grow so they can learn to be, do, and have more. When we stop growing, we stop advancing. Author Mark Sanborn said, "The test of leadership is, is anything or anyone better because of you?"

Let me give some real-life examples of intentional team growth. Several prominent organizations that I've had the opportunity to work with challenged their staff to read the same leadership de-

41

velopment book together each month. They used the book as their topic of discussion during their weekly staff meetings to continually improve their skills and implement better techniques. One organization I've worked with gives financial rewards to employees for every leadership book read and reported on. In an effort to foster personal growth, they also rewarded team members who attended leadership conferences. Another organization I know gives professional development credits for any extracurricular programs their employees accomplish, knowing these programs expand skills within the company. The more credits received, the more incentives there are to cash in on. These incentives come in the form of extra vacation time, special bonuses, an assortment of gifts, and so on.

Most successful companies provide outside coaching opportunities for their employees. This is one of the best ways to let your leaders have a personal coach that is helping draw out the potential within them. An internal report of the Personnel Management Association showed that when training is combined with coaching, individuals increase their productivity by an average of 86%, compared to 22% with training alone. I work with many different organizations that are investing into their leaders by bringing me in as their leadership coach and we see huge improvements in performance as a result. These are just a few examples of intentionally creating time for your team to grow. Whatever you decide to do, make sure you are making it a priority for your team to sharpen their skills.

2) Invest In Growth

You have to see developing your people as a pivotal investment. Growing up around the farmlands of southern Indiana, I know the only way to reap a great harvest in the fall is to devote time for planting in the spring. Invest the seeds of opportunity in your team today, and you will reap great dividends in the future. When you invest in your people, you directly invest into the quality of your organization. As a leader, it's imperative that you provide financial allotments for your team's growth. An organization that does not have a budget for development is an organization that will eventually not have a budget to sustain itself.

People are the ones who create products, and people are the ones who buy products. Your products and services are only as good as the people developing them. Sadly, one of the first items to get cut in many organizations' budget is the professional development fund, if they even had one at all. Ironically, development should be one of the most important line items in the budget of an organization. Make sure you are setting aside finances and resources for personal and professional growth to occur in your organization. Invest in opportunities for your team to be equipped with the right tools for their skills. The more you invest in their growth, the more compounded interest you will gain from the investment. Showing your team that you care about their development communicates that you value them. When a team member feels they are worth the investment, they tend to live up to that investment. In the 1960s, an employee from IBM made a monumental, ten-million-dollar mistake. To make his emotional instability worse, he then had to tell the CEO, Thomas

J. Watson, what he had done. He walked into Mr. Watson's office expecting to get fired on the spot.

"Fire you?" Mr. Watson asked. "I just spent ten million dollars educating you!" This person was not only relieved, but empowered as well. Great leaders invest into their team to make them the best.

3) Never Stop Growing

Albert Einstein said, "Intellectual growth should commence at birth and cease only at death." One night my family and I were sitting at the dinner table eating our meal together and sharing stories from our day. My daughter asked me what I had done at work. I told her I had the opportunity to speak to a large group of business leaders about leadership. Confused, she looked at me and laughed while saying, "But, Daddy, they're ALREADY leaders!" She thought I had made a big mistake and spoke to the wrong group.

Many people think like my daughter did. They have the misconception that once you receive the title of "leader," your growth is over. It's the temptation to think you've arrived and no longer need to develop yourself. This type of thinking couldn't be further from the truth. The moment you are endowed with the title of

> "Only when we admit that we don't know it all can we open the door to unlimited possibilities."

"leader" is the perfect moment to begin growing your skills all the more. Once you get something, that doesn't mean you've got it; it means you now need to grow it. I like how Coach John Wooden put it when he said, "It's what you learn after you know it all that counts." Only when we admit that we don't know it all can we open the door to unlimited possibilities. At age 94, Pablo Casals was considered one of the greatest cellists of all time. After one of his last concerts at the Kennedy Center in Washington D.C. he was asked why he still practiced over three hours a day. He responded, "I think I am making progress." He also stated, "To retire is the beginning of death." Always push your team to stay in a growth mindset. Challenge them to get better and better and to never settle for where they currently are.

Everyone wants to get better, but few are willing to pay the price to do so. Sadly, many people live their lives waiting to stumble into success. These people believe success is a destination that can be reached. But waiting is not a strategy and success is not a landmark. People do not go to success as though it is waiting for them somewhere; they grow into success by developing their skills day by day. The only way to become successful in life is to practice successful growth habits. You become what you habitually practice. Habits shape us, for better or worse.

Here are some growth habits to develop into your life and your team:

Learn From Reading

No one will ever grow to their maximum potential without reading. Reading great books, stories, biographies, articles, and blogs pertaining to your area of interest is one of the fastest ways to grow on your journey. Take the wisdom and insights offered from others and apply it to your situation. To transform, the mind needs stimulation. One of the best ways to stimulate the mind is to read. It lets you soar on the wings of other people's great ideas and insights. Leaders are readers. Books are to the mind what nutrition is to the body. The more you dive into great books, the more growth you'll experience. American philosopher Mortimer Jerome Adler said, "In the case of good books, the point is not how many of them you can get through, but rather how many can get through to you." If you want inspiration, simply read. If you want information, study what you read. If you want transformation, act on what you read.

Learn From Educated Experiences

Experience is not the best teacher; educated experience is. It is not enough to simply go through situations; you have to grow through situations. Just because someone goes through a difficult time does not necessarily mean they automatically learned from it. We all know people who have gone through a lot but have nothing to show from it. Educating yourself as to what you have acquired through your experiences will give you incredible insight into the future.

> "It's not what we've experienced that shapes us; it's what we've learned from our experiences that truly shape us."

It's not what we've experienced that shapes us; it's what we've learned from our experiences that truly shape us. Unless we help people take the time

46

to reflect, they will be destined to repeat the past, or worse, forget about it. Every experience brings with it a seed of success. Don't allow your team to waste experiences. Instead, help them to cultivate growth lessons from their experiences. Vernon Howard said, "Always walk through life as if you have something new to learn and you will."

Learn From Other People

You can learn most everything you need in life by being around the right people. Finding mentors who will lift you to a higher level is vital for success. People become like those they surround themselves with. What kind of people are you surrounding yourself with? What kind of people is your team surrounded with? Successful people are drawn to other successful people. They intentionally seek out those who are better and further along than they are themselves. One of the greatest traits of highly successful people is the drive to find and learn from people who are good at what they do. They go the extra mile to network with experts. We cannot reach our potential alone; we need others to help draw the best out of us. Get your people around great people.

Creating a growth environment requires upkeep and tending—just like a Bonsai tree. If left unattended, the weeds of apathy and stagnation begin to choke out progress. In order for your team to be equipped with a growth mindset, you must make it a priority to create an ongoing culture of development. Every team has a culture and that culture is a reflection of the leader's beliefs and behaviors. This means you have to first model a passion for personal and professional growth. Don't expect your team to grow if you are not intentionally growing yourself. An organization's culture is formed from the top down. When the team sees the importance of growth from their leaders, they will see the value in it for themselves. Novelist Oliver Goldsmith once said, "People seldom improve when they have no other model but themselves to copy." The more you model a growth mindset, the faster your organization will mature into a fruitful Bonsai tree.

Questions To Think About:

A) How does your organization develop leaders currently?

_____

_____

_____

B) How can you incorporate more incentive for growth opportunities on your team(s)?

_____

_____

_____

C) List three ways you are going to intentionally grow yourself and your team in the next six months.

1._____

_____

2._____

_____

3._____

_____

Leadology Challenge:

If I asked you, "What is your growth plan?" What would the response be? Would you be able to give me a quick and precise answer? If you hesitate or have to think hard about it, I have bad news for you…you probably don't have a growth plan. The most successful companies and leaders know exactly what they are doing to help develop their people. They have thought through the process and implemented a system that creates a greenhouse effect of growth. They are able to tell you what it is very quickly and precisely because of the effort they have put into it.

You should have a specific growth plan for yourself, and your team should have a specific growth plan for themselves. Take some time to sit down and create a plan for how you are going to grow, or, if you already have a growth plan, sit down and reassess to see if there is anything you need to update within it. I would also encourage you to theme out your growth plan around the specific areas you want to improve in. For example, if better communication is the topic of growth, rally around resources, speakers, conferences, leadership coaches, lunch & learns, anything that will help develop communication skills. Do this for a few months as you keep the topic in the forefront of your focus. Always be investing into your leadership greenhouse.

The GAS Tank

|| Idea #3 ||

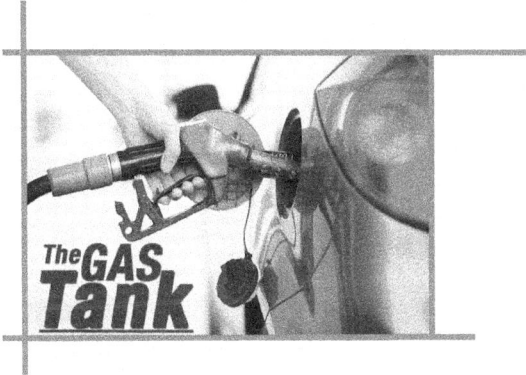

The Gas Tank

Leaders are always finding creative ways to accelerate their team's progress. The more a leader can do to generate momentum, the further the team will go. Motivating others is a key component to success, and it must be practiced daily.

I will never forget when I first got my driver's license. It's the pinnacle moment in a teenager's life when independence becomes tangible. Dreaming of cruising the open road with my friends took up most of my time—and not just cruising, but cruising in style; driving a beast of a machine down the road, making everybody's head turn. My beast turned out to be a 1988 blue Ford Escort. I squeezed my bank account dry and paid eight hundred dollars for my smooth ride. It may not have been the red Lamborghini that a teenage boy dreams of, but I was so proud of that car.

With a new car came new responsibilities. It was time to get a job to pay for all of this new independence. So I decided to spread my wings that summer and move to the city to work a job that paid more than I could make in my small hometown. Of course, still being in high school, I needed a roommate while in the city. I was feeling the freedom now. My blue Escort, a job in the city, making more money than I ever had before, a roommate…my grandma. While living with Grandma that summer, I worked at a carpet warehouse that a friend of mine set me up with. The warehouse was a pretty good distance from Grandma's house, and I learned that long commutes can become monotonous and a burden on my gas tank. Gas may have been cheap back then, but it wasn't cheap for a teenager; even a teenager with a job in the city. So one day after work I decided to break up the monotony and find a shorter way to drive back to Grandmas and hopefully conserve some gas—my first mistake.

I didn't know my way around the city very well, but I thought I could rely on my superb navigational skills—my second mistake. A trip that should have taken me twenty-five minutes turned into a three-hour tour of the greater metropolitan area. Typical male tendencies kicked in early in my life and I decided that I didn't want to stop and ask for directions—my third mistake. I reasoned that if I got myself into this mess, I could get myself out of it. If I could just give it a little more time surely something would start to look familiar. If this had been modern day, I would have simply pulled out my cell phone and used my GPS, but these were pre-cell phone days, and there was no Siri to help me navigate through this problem.

By this point in the journey, my fourth and biggest mistake was beginning to become clear to me. In all of my scheming to find a way to conserve my precious fuel, I had forgotten to check my gas gauge before I left work. If I had, I would have seen the need for a fill-up. Fast-forward a few hours and by now I was riding on fumes. The bad thing was that my wallet was running on fumes too—no green to be seen. I was a teenager, so I didn't have a debit card or any other means of payment. I had no way at all to get any money. As the panic was starting to set in, I noticed a payphone up ahead. I searched every crack and crevice of my car hoping to find loose change to make my call but came up with nothing. Staring out the window, debating on what to do, I spotted my hope of getting out of this mess: a homeless man just a few feet from the payphone.

I got out of my car and asked if I could bum a quarter off of him. He obviously felt I needed it more than he did, and he gave me a quarter. I called Grandma, and thankfully she answered. She arranged for a friend of hers that lived nearby to bring me gas and help me get home. Problem solved thanks to a homeless man and my first roommate. I learned many lessons that day, but the one that sticks out the most is: it takes a lot of gas if you want to keep going.

> "When *what* we do is aligned with *wanting* to do it, there is momentum."

Just like my car ran out of gas, people too, run out of motivational gas if they aren't consistently having their tanks filled. Teams will lose momentum if leaders fail to inspire them. Motivation is the fuel that drives productivity. When *what* we do is aligned with *wanting* to do it, there is momentum. One of my good friends, Chris Page, says, "Burnout occurs when your mind is committed to something your heart is not in." Leaders bridge the gap between the head and the heart.

If you look closely, you will find that each day will present you with defining moments of opportunity to motivate your team. In the times before modern harbors, a sailor had to wait for the flood tide before they could make it to port with their ship. The Latin phrase "Ob Portu" referred to that moment in time when the tide turned. The captain and crew would wait for that one moment, knowing that if they missed it, they would have to wait for another tide to come in. The English word *opportunity* derives from this original meaning. Shakespeare used this idea of "Ob Portu" in one of his most famous passages from *Julius Caesar*:

> *There is a tide in the affairs of men,*
> *Which, taken at the flood, leads on to fortune;*
> *Omitted, all the voyage of their life*
> *Is bound in shallows and in miseries.*
> *On such a full sea are we now afloat;*
> *And we must take the current when it serves,*
> *Or lose our ventures.*

Great leaders are always looking for ways to link daily duties to the overarching vision. They connect every dot to its purpose.

They are continuously searching for waves of opportunity to ride. Sometimes these waves of opportunity come in the form of sharing wins for the company at a staff meeting. Sometimes it's in publicly praising a team member who closed a critical sale. Sometimes, it's as simple as connecting a testimonial from a customer with the overall vision of the organization. Other times it may be rewarding those who have gone above and beyond the call of duty.

Every little opportunity eventually generates big breakthroughs. Don't let yourself become so busy that you miss moments to fill your team's motivational tank. You have to be the most vocal cheerleader for your people and your cause. You lead the best when you cheer the loudest. Leaders spark hope and enthusiasm in others. Many people have no one around who truly believes in them. They travel through life without anyone to push them on and challenge them to live up to their potential. It is difficult enough for people to believe in themselves when others *do* believe in them, so imagine how hard it is for someone to believe in themselves when they feel *no one* believes in them. Businessman Harvey MacKay said, "If you wish others to believe in you, you must first convince them that you believe in them."

The most powerful way to motivate someone and fill their emotional tank is to encourage them. Encouragement is an irresistible form of inspiration. The word *encourage* is a compound of the prefix *EN*, meaning to put in or into; and the word *courage*, meaning confidence and strength. To "*encourage*" literally means to put courage into someone. When courage resides in someone's heart, they are bolder, stronger, and more effective in all that they do. Their bravery will push them to overcome any obstacle that may stand in their way. Courage conquers fear and motivates an individual to do things they never thought possible. Hope gives people the possibility of a greater future and encouragement gives them the strength to go after it. Olympic weightlifter, author, and speaker, Jim Stovell, said, "You need to be aware of what others are doing, applaud their efforts, acknowledge their successes, and encourage them in their pursuits. When we all help one another, everyone wins."

> "Hope gives people the possibility of a greater future and encouragement gives them the strength to go after it."

It has been said that:

The five most important words are: "I have confidence in you."

The four most important words are: "What is your opinion?"

The three most important words are: "If you please."

The two most important words are: "Thank you."

The most important word is: "We."

The least important word is: "I."

Encouraging others takes the focus off of you and places it on another. When people are recognized and valued, it puts wind in the sails of their future. The more encouragement one receives from you, the more he or she will open up. Leadership is only effective when relationships are developed through genuinely positive interactions. People are much more willing to listen to you and trust you when they have an encouraging relationship with you. Making encouragement a priority in your communication will open up a direct line of connection. William Arthur Ward said, "Flatter me, and I may not believe you. Criticize me, and I may not like you. Ignore me, and I may not forgive you. Encourage me, and I will not forget you." People are more influenced by those who consistently encourage them than by those who consistently criticize them. A leader who expects their team to stay motivated without intentionally filling the motivational tank will find the team's engine stalled.

There are three truths we always need to keep in mind regarding motivation:

1) Everyone Is Motivated By Something

In 1981, multi-millionaire Eugene Lang greatly changed the lives of a sixth-grade class in East Harlem. Mr. Lang had been asked to speak to a class of sixty-one sixth-graders. What could he say to inspire these students, most of who would drop out of school? He wondered how he could get these predominantly African-American and Puerto Rican children to look even at him.

Scrapping his notes, he decided to speak to them from his heart. "Stay in school," he said. "And I'll help pay the college tuition for every one of you." At that moment, the countenance of these students changed. For the first time, they had hope, and it motivated them. One student remarked, "I had something to look forward to, something waiting for me. It was a golden feeling." In fact, Mr. Lang went further than just donating money. He created programs to keep them college-bound by providing tutors, field trips to colleges, an open door to his office, and, most importantly, his encouragement. Nearly 90% of that class went on to graduate from high school.

Eugene Lang motivated those sixth-graders to be and do more. There is no such thing as an "unmotivated" person; just people who haven't found what their motivation is yet. Everyone is motivated by something. Whenever I see an "unmotivated" person, I always wonder what it would take for them to be inspired. I ask myself, "What would drive them to move forward?" Many times, leaders are at a loss when it comes to knowing how to motivate others because they haven't taken the proper time to find out what drives them. If you can't figure it out, don't be afraid to sit down and simply ask the person what their motivation is. This will give you great insight that will help you spur them on.

2) Everyone Is Motivated Differently

Everyone on your team has a different motivational style. Many leaders think that motivation is a one size fits all thing. This isn't the case. Some people are motivated by external goals and tangible results while others are more internally motivated by feelings, emotion, purpose, and significance. Neither person is right or wrong; they just each have their unique motivational style. Some people are motivated by stability, predictability, and security. Others are motivated by multitasking, risk taking, and high-pressure environments. Again, neither is right or wrong; it's just unique to the individual.

Leaders have to know the personality type of whom they are

dealing with to know how to motivate them. If a leader pushes a stability-driven person into high-risk and high-pressure work environments, that person is going to become highly unmotivated. In the same way, if a high-pressure driven multitasker is put in a predictable and slow environment, then they are going to lose their motivation to produce as well. The key is to know what type of person you are dealing with. A leader must study their team to know all their unique motivational styles. When a leader comes to know the team, they are a major step closer to figuring out how to get the best out of them.

A common mistake a leader can make is trying to motivate their team solely by using tactics that motivate them personally. Just because you, as the leader, are motivated a certain way does not mean that others on your team will be motivated in that same way. If the leader only motivates others based on their personal style, they will alienate the other motivational styles team members have. That leader will become frustrated, thinking that their team is being ungrateful, when, in reality, the leader is failing to understand the motivation of the individuals on the team.

Study your team and be aware of what drives your people. Make notes, file ideas, and reflect on each to get the best from them. I once knew a leader who kept a file for each one of his employees. In that file, he would write down notes and spend time studying that person's motivations so he was able to know truly how to utilize everyone to their fullest potential. He was very successful at it. And it was well worth the time and energy it took to be in tune with his team.

3) Everyone Needs Motivated Daily

Zig Ziglar said, "People often say that motivation doesn't last. Well, neither does bathing—that's why we recommend it daily." Motivation is a well that runs dry very quickly if not replenished often. While working with one organization, I began

> "Motivation is a well that runs dry very quickly if not replenished often."

coaching one of the top-level leaders who was responsible for all of the operation managers in the company. He had become increasingly frustrated at the low morale of his team. He felt they had lost their drive to move the company forward. He wasn't sure if they were the right fit anymore.

As we began to uncover the problem, we, in fact, discovered that *he* was the problem. This leader had failed to develop the morale of his team. He expected them to have automatic enthusiasm without having to be involved in the process. Thinking that an annual team-building meeting would supply enough encouragement for the other eleven months caused his team to run out of gas. He came to realize that his team was suffering from what I call "affirmation deprivation." He viewed encouragement as a leadership event, not a leadership lifestyle.

But the truth is, it's a lifestyle. People need affirmation on a consistent basis in one way or another. This leader began to see how he had neglected the responsibility to be there for his team. He was so caught up in doing what he needed to do, that he forgot to be what his team needed him to be. Instead of being distant from them he started to develop them by spending time building their courage through specific affirmation. This had a dramatic effect on the morale of his team. They began to feel needed, valued, and united, which increased their enthusiasm to be more productive. He now has made it a habit to walk through the halls in his company looking for ways to build his team up whenever he can.

While on a conference call with my mentor, Dr. John C. Maxwell, I was able to learn about a conversation that impacted him greatly. During a dinner with Truett Cathy, the founder of Chik-fil-A, Truett looked at John and said, "Do you know how to tell if someone needs encouragement?"
John asked, "How?"
He quickly responded, "That person is breathing."

This nugget of truth that Dr. Maxwell gleaned during a dinner meeting is the same nugget the leader I mentioned in the story above learned. People need motivation like they need the air they breathe. It's a necessity, not a luxury.

Canlis is one of the best fine dining restaurant in the world. It is located in Seattle and has been around since 1950. It is known for impeccable customer service. Guests come from all over, trusting the staff with their special moment—whether it's a proposal, a special celebration, or even the last meal a family may have together because of a terminal illness. Canlis masterfully creates an unforgettable experience for their guests during these special moments they are sharing. A tradition they've held to over the years is a pre-dinner service huddle with the whole staff before show time. The team gathers together in a circle on the dinning room floor and repeats the mantra "KEEP THE PROMISE."

They remind their staff to keep the promise by delivering the best dining experience their guests will ever receive. In fact, that saying is something they post on the wall of the restaurant for all to see. Owner Brian Canlis said, "Keeping the promise is ensuring guests come first with what is fragile and precious to them on that particular evening. How dare we put ourselves in the spotlight when what is important for our guests is what is on their minds and hearts when they come." Canlis truly knows what it takes to keep their team motivated to be the best each day they come to work.

We can never tire of giving encouragement to others. It is an unending commitment that produces highly motivated people. The more you fill the motivational tank of your team the further they can go.

Questions To Think About:

A) Describe when you and/or your team have been the most motivated in the past?

_____

_____

_____

B) What motivates you more than any other factor?

_____

_____

_____

C) What would it take for you and/or your team to keep motivated daily?

_____

_____

_____

Leadology Challenge:

We have all experienced motivational moments we didn't expect—forces that drove us to dig in and make things happen. These times sometimes even take us by surprise, and we suddenly feel "in the zone." It's what psychologist Mihály Csíkszentmihályi famously called, "Flow."

But instead of waiting for these moments to suddenly appear in our day, we need to learn how to generate momentum on command. As leaders, we need to connect the dots of purpose, passion, and personality to what needs to be done. When people are operating in their sweet spot they have these moments of flow, where work just seems to smoothly take off. Make a list of each of your team members or key leaders, and figure out how to get yourself and each member in this flow momentum. When you take the time to know each person's motivation, you can almost trigger momentum on command. Know your team. Know their motivations. You may need to sit down with each member and have some deep conversations to figure out what makes them feel alive when they're at work. Simply ask them what fills their motivational tank.

Take the same inventory of yourself. Do as Socrates taught and "know thyself." You can't generate momentum if you don't know what puts gas in your own tank. Spend some time in self-awareness and make a list of the things that drive you.

The Goose Duck

The Goose Duck

The most important person you will ever lead is yourself. Leadership is more about who you are than what you do. What you are doing is not as important as who you are becoming. Your actions will either solidify your claims or sabotage your credibility.

Our family loves history. We take any opportunity we have to learn more about the life and times before us. Our family also loves to have fun. So when we heard about an amazing little town that was combining history and fun into a Canal Days Festival, we jumped at the chance to visit. My wife and I loaded our daughters into the car and off we went. The Canal Days Festival was a huge celebration of the history of horse-drawn canal boats. These canal boats fueled the Southeastern Indiana economy until the railroad replaced them.

The highlight of our day was when we actually got to take a boat ride down the famous canal. Along the route we passed the Duck Creek Aqueduct, a covered bridge that carries the canal sixteen feet over Duck Creek. It is believed to be the only structure of its kind in the nation. It was pretty amazing to experience that with my family, but the most interesting part of the boat ride happened when we reached the other side of the bridge. After emerging from the aqueduct, I noticed a large group of ducks walking around the bank; very fitting for Duck Creek. But I also noticed something else. Among all of these ducks was one peculiar-looking creature strolling along with them: A goose.

Our tour guide began explaining this interesting flock to us. He pointed the goose out and said that for years the bird had been following the ducks wherever they went. Every time the boat passes by the area, the ducks and the lone goose start to waddle around the bank of the canal. The guide also went on to tell us that over the years, the goose had started to walk like the ducks and adopt their mannerisms. It was amazing to watch as this goose literally waddled around while it followed the ducks' lead. The goose forgot it was a goose and had grown up to think it was a duck.

But it was obvious to everyone that saw it, that even though this bird acted like a duck, it was definitely a goose. The image of this goose stuck in my mind for the rest of our visit. Who knew that the most impactful thing in this entire day filled with history and fun would be a goose who tried to act like a duck?

After the festival, I began to wonder how a goose could completely forget what it was created to be. It made me realize that, just like the goose, people can lose their true identity by trying to be something or someone they're not. Being authentic is essential to becoming a great leader and maximizing influence with others. Leaders lead best by setting a legitimate example for their team. The "do as I say, not as I do" mentality never works; period. You must lead with your actions as well as your words. People do what people see. Your team will be a reflection of your image.

Just like the goose following the ducks, your people will follow your lead. Being an example is about actively demonstrating your values, behaviors, and beliefs, not just talking about them. Albert Schweitzer said, "Example is not the main thing in influencing others; it is the only thing." Who you are is what your people will eventually become. People will naturally shape into the model their leader is building. As goes the leader's attitude and outlook, so goes the team's attitude and outlook. Leaders will always reproduce who they are in their followers, for better or worse.

If you do not like what you see in your people, you may need to change the way you are leading yourself. Theodore Roosevelt once stated, "If you could kick the person

> "If you do not like what you see in your people, you may need to change the way you are leading yourself."

in the pants responsible for most of your trouble, you wouldn't sit for a month." We cannot expect to challenge others if we are not challenging ourselves. If we are having trouble motivating ourselves, we will have an extremely hard time motivating others. You can't lead the masses if you can't lead yourself.

The reason I truly have a passion for leadership is because I believe the quality of a person's life depends on their ability to lead themselves. I remember the desire I had to learn more about leadership as a young adult. It was not a desire driven by a want for position or authority over others; it was a desire that was birthed from my deep passion and dedication to lead myself and make a positive impact in the world. When I began to study and learn about leadership, I discovered that it was more about me than it was the masses. I started to devour any and every resource I could get my hands on to help me guide my life.

At the time, I didn't have the income, networking, knowhow, or in some cases the time machine that I needed in order to meet people like Norman Vincent Peale, Napoleon Hill, Dale Carnegie, Dr. Stephen Covey, Dr. John C. Maxwell, Jim Collins, and a host of others. So, I used the one resource I did have available to me: books. I even took a side job at a bookstore, because I wanted to be surrounded by great books. I studied these leaders' resources and teachings and it shaped my paradigm.

I still remember listening to every Zig Ziglar tape (yes, I said tape, as in cassette) as a young twenty-year-old working a side job as a janitor of a dialyses center in Maryville, Tennessee. I would clock in around midnight, pop in my Ziglar tape, and start cleaning. I listened to the same tapes night after night until I literally memorized every one of them. The dialysis center paid me to clean, but during those hours of cleaning I was truly earning hundreds of credit hours towards a self-worth leadership degree. The principles I learned while cleaning the center directed the course of my career and inspired my devotion to personal development. Since that time, I have been on my own journey of leading prominent teams, organizations, and individuals down their own path of leadership development.

And it all started with a desire to lead myself first.

The more authentic we are, the greater our influence becomes. What we say and what we do must be aligned in order to establish credibility and respect. Never let the external pressure distract you from your internal purpose. To be an authentic leader we must start with three foundational actions:

1) Honor Those Above You

During the holidays, my family and I were watching *A Charlie Brown Christmas*. In one of my favorite clips, Lucy approaches Charlie Brown and says, "Merry Christmas, Charlie Brown. 'Tis the season of peace on earth and good will toward men.' Therefore, I suggest we forget our differences and love one another."

At this, Charlie Brown responds, "That's wonderful, Lucy. I'm so glad you said that. But tell me, do we have to love each other only at this season of the year? Why can't we love each other all year long?"

To which Lucy responds, "What are you, some kind of fanatic or something?"

Like Lucy, we sometimes think it's unrealistic to truly live in peace and good will with everyone. My generation, and those behind me, have unfortunately done a great job at removing the concept of honor, especially in regard to those in authority over them. They have confused honor with respect and have come to believe it's something they can withhold based on the performance or likability of the person they're accrediting it to. Although respect must be earned, honor should be freely given from the start. Choosing to honor those around you will reciprocate honor right back to you.

You will never be credible in the eyes of others if you are bad-mouthing your superiors. If you are speaking negatively about your leaders, you can be sure to expect your team to do the same to you behind your back. Remember the saying, "What goes around comes around?" That statement is truer than you may think. But the great news is this law can also work for the good when utilized properly.

> "Protecting the reputation and character of those above you builds a strong foundation of support underneath you."

Protecting the reputation and character of those above you builds a strong foundation of support underneath you.

Give honor to your organization and the people you serve under by speaking highly of them. Speak about your superiors the way you would want them to speak about you. If you can follow this simple step, you will always live honorably. Growing up, I remember my mom teaching me the Golden Rule. The Golden Rule says, "Do to others what you would have them do to you." I thought my mom had things twisted around. I reasoned it was her old age confusing her memory.

"Poor mom," I thought to myself, "she keeps saying it wrong. Somebody should tell her she's really lost it." It took me a long time to understand that I was the one who had it twisted, and, in fact, my wise mother was right all along. My natural tendency was to want others to do unto me what I wanted them to do for me. My Golden Rule had become increasingly tarnished.

But over time I realized that when you help others and honor them, they would most likely do the same for you. Remember this: You have to give honor to live honorably. This Golden Rule applies to every area of life, including leadership. Think of the Golden Rule in these terms: Do unto "others" as though you were the "others." Mary Kay Ash said, "We treat our people like royalty. If you honor and serve the people who work for you, they will honor and serve you." When you genuinely speak well of others, others will genuinely speak well of you.

2) Be Willing To Jump In And S.E.R.V.E.

Authentic leaders are willing to help out wherever they can for the success of the team. The worst statement that can be made by someone is, "That's not in my job description." No task is "below" a great leader. If you think serving is below you, then leadership is beyond you. Always remember that leadership is not something you do *to* people, it's something you are doing *for* them. Eleanor Roosevelt said, "It is not fair to ask of others what you are not willing to do yourself."

> "Always remember that leadership is not something you do *to* people, it's something you are doing *for* them."

One of the best examples a leader can set is one of genuine teamwork that is expressed by serving those they lead. Look out for others by being willing to do tasks necessary and possibly out of your job description to push the team forward. Leaders exist to serve people—not to make people serve them. Robert Greenleaf, the founder of the modern servant leadership movement and the Greenleaf Center for Servant Leadership, said, "Good leaders must first become good servants."

Leaders S.E.R.V.E. others by making it…

S = Simple

Don't make it hard to be a servant. Don't wait to do *everything* before you do *something*. If you wait to do *something* until you can do *everything*, you won't do *anything*. Just start with what you can do. It's not always the big things that make the biggest difference. Sometimes it's the small things that have the greatest impact. I have heard that little termites do more physical damage in a year's time than all natural disasters combined. Small acts of kindness and service go a long way. Serving doesn't have to be complicated or monumental; it just needs to be genuine.

E = Exciting

Don't serve with a frown on your face or a bad attitude. Nothing is worse than someone who is helping but doesn't really want to. If you're going to serve others, be excited about the opportunity to lift them up. Don't walk around complaining about what you are doing for others. Find the purpose in why you are serving and keep your eyes on the bigger picture: people. Showing an excitement to help others makes them feel valuable.

R = Random

Random means there is no organized process; it's just spontaneous. Step out when you see a need. Serve others when they are least expecting it and when you are least expecting it. I am sure it means a lot to you when someone drops what they are doing to randomly help you, so return the favor. If you see a need, be the one to fill it. Spontaneous, genuine help impacts people. The less they expect it, the bigger the impact it makes. Random acts of kindness result in specific acts of gratitude.

V = Voluntary

Be the one to step up and take the initiative to serve. Do it without expecting anything in return. Volunteer yourself without being forced or required to. The word *volunteer* is defined as a person who does some act or enters into a transaction without being under any legal obligation to do so and without being promised any remuneration for his services. Volunteers serve from the heart. John Bunyan said, "You have not lived today unless you've done something for someone who can never repay you."

E = Enduring

Don't stop serving. I have met many leaders who feel they have "paid their dues" and no longer need to serve. They think they've somehow grown out of the servant role. But you never move beyond being a servant no matter what level you may be on. It is not something you do for a season and then graduate from. Serving is a life-long endeavor; it is a lifestyle of valuing people.

Don't grow weary from serving. It is hard work and will require blood, sweat, and even tears at times. Don't stop because of the effort it takes. The payoff from serving far outweighs the comfort of sitting. It takes humility to surrender your selfishness and energy. No doubt we need to pace ourselves and be careful of those who "use" us, but better to lean on the side of serving than the side of selfishness.

Author Gordon MacDonald said, "You can tell whether you are becoming a servant by how you act when you're treated like one." Make it a point to serve someone every day and your influence will grow stronger and stronger because of it.

3) Set Your Own Expectations

Businessman Ray Kroc said, "The quality of a leader is reflected in the standards they set for themselves." The most effective form of leadership is to exemplify the high expectations you set on others.

It's said that one-day, Frederick the Great of Prussia was walking on the outskirts of Berlin when he encountered a very old man walking ramrod-straight in the opposite direction.

"Who are you?" Frederick asked his subject.

"I am a king," replied the old man.

"A king!" laughed Frederick. "Over what kingdom do you reign?"

"Over myself," was the proud old man's reply.

You are responsible for yourself. The expectations you set on yourself should outdo the expectations others have of you. We don't see things as *they* are, we see things as *we* are, so, if you constantly degrade yourself, you will have a hard time reaching your fullest potential. If you are constantly thinking poorly of yourself, you will always be discouraged. Philosopher Lao Tzu said, "He who conquers others is strong; he who conquers himself is mighty."

Remember these truths:
- ✓ To be an influential leader you have to believe in your potential.
- ✓ You will never enjoy life to the fullest if you don't challenge yourself to be your best.
- ✓ You have to value yourself if you want to find value in what you do.
- ✓ You need to be your biggest fan, greatest motivator, and loudest cheerleader.
- ✓ If you don't value yourself, don't expect others to place a high value on you either.

✓ Do not presume you'll get the most out of life if you don't get the most out of yourself.

✓ The greatest opinion we have is the opinion we have of ourselves.

✓ How you see yourself is how you will see the world around you.

✓ You will never outperform the way you view yourself.

✓ You have to see value in who you are before you can add value to others.

Expect yourself to be a person of passion, purpose, and possibilities in all that you do. You were created for more than you can imagine. You were designed to offer this world something very special. And only you have the ability to take what you've been given and use it for good. Never bury your potential because you've believed the lie that you are not important. Zig Ziglar said, "You were born to win, but to be a winner, you must plan to win, prepare to win, and expect to win." Set your expectations high and you will rise to that level. Be the best version of yourself.

> "Be the best version of yourself."

Authenticity can be an overused and underestimated word. But great leaders never allow themselves to forget its power. The bigger the gap between who you are and what you do; the smaller your leadership becomes.

In other words, don't be a goose duck!

Questions To Think About:

A) What does the word "authenticity" mean to you?

_____

_____

_____

B) What expectations do you set on yourself?

_____

_____

_____

C) List three ways you can increase serving those around you.

1._____

_____

2._____

_____

3._____

_____

Leadology Challenge:

Every day you bring a version of yourself to work. It's your choice who that person will be. It will either be the best version of yourself, the worst version of yourself, or the caught-in-the-middle version of yourself. Chances are that different situations cause a different version of yourself to appear. But to be truly successful, we need to strive to bring the boldest, most focused, and energized version of ourselves to all that we do. It's when we are truly present that we become a great leader.

When we approach each day with a bold, collective, and strong self-image, we relax our body chemistry, which allows us to think clearly and navigate tactfully. The more uncomfortable we feel, the more we release high levels of cortisol in our body, which is the stress hormone. The more that cortisol rises in the moment, the more confused and muddy our thinking becomes. This is why we forget simple things in fearful situations. To bring our best self to meetings and challenges, we need to practice the art of opening up our body language and getting ourselves into a confident state of mind. Social Psychologist Amy Cuddy says, "Focus less on the impression you're making on others and more on the impression you're making on yourself." When your own self-image is strong you come across as confident and inspiring. This means you have to truly love yourself…I know it sounds mushy…but it is VERY true. I don't mean love yourself in an arrogant way, but in a healthy, self-confident way.

The Pink Flamingo

|| Idea #5 ||

The Pink Flamingo

Teamwork multiplies your effort. One can accomplish much, but two can accomplish much more. Three, even more, and four, well...you get the point. Building a great team will determine how far your impact will go.

When our two daughters were younger, we surprised them with a family vacation to Walt Disney World. We had an enchanting experience enjoying the sheer magic of Disney. Not only did we have a blast riding the rides, meeting characters, eating at fun restaurants, and seeing great shows, but we also learned so much. Disney not only values amusement; it also emphasizes education.

One of the things I remember learning was a fascinating fact about pink flamingos. While in the Animal Kingdom, I was mesmerized watching these beautiful creatures walk, run, and eat. But what really caught my attention was a group of flamingos standing very still on one leg with the other leg curled up. This was an amazing sight, because if you've ever seen a pink flamingo you know their legs aren't much more than tiny straws when compared with the rest of their body. I couldn't believe that one teeny-tiny leg could support all of their weight. These birds stood still as statues, not flinching a muscle. I assumed they were trying to get some yoga training in while the day was still young, but I went ahead and asked the tour guide what the true reason was. Her answer was simply, "They like it." She told me that flamingos stand on one leg when they sleep, when they rise, and really anytime they want to. They simply like it, but no one really knows why. Go figure.

It's a mystery to scientists exactly why flamingos spend so much time on one leg. It's an amazing feat when you notice their legs are so much longer than their bodies, and that their body is designed like a horizontal weight balancing on top of these skinny sticks. People, on the other hand, have their weight distributed vertically, lining up with the center of gravity. So because of this, one would think it would be easier for people to stand on one leg than our pink-feathered friends. But anyone who has gone leg-to-leg with a flamingo in a balancing contest knows this isn't true. We would all agree that it is much easier to stand on two legs. The more support we have, the better off we are, unless you are a flamingo of course.

Think about these dynamic duos that just seem to be better together than standing alone:

- Peanut Butter & Jelly
- Macaroni & Cheese

- Salt & Pepper
- Cake & Ice cream
- Dora & Diego
- Love & Marriage
- Pen & Paper
- Lock & Key
- Romeo & Juliet
- Nuts & Bolts

Each of these things needs the other to make a great combination. We're better together when it comes to most everything, which is why teamwork is essential. Immense research has shown that if someone is in community with other like-minded people who are pursuing the same goal the chances of success dramatically increase. This is why weight loss groups see such great results. The reality is, we can't stand alone in leadership. When we stand alone we are more vulnerable to being knocked over. We can't succeed to the fullest on our own; we need each other.

The Lone Ranger is a great western hero, but the Lone Ranger is just a myth. The Lone Ranger or Rambo-type personalities don't work in thriving organizations. In fact, the Lone Ranger wasn't even that alone anyway. He had his sidekick, Tonto, to help him. When Tonto wasn't there to help, things didn't turn out so well. Like the time when the Ranger and Tonto were surrounded by a group of hostile Indians and it seemed that defeat was eminent for the two, the Lone Ranger looked at his long trusted partner and said, "Tonto, we must fight brave and fast or we will die!"

Tonto thought about the predicament, then looked at the Pale Ranger and replied, "What you mean, *we*, white man?"

The Lone Ranger is not reality. In the real world, extraordinary accomplishments are the result of a team working together for a common purpose. The better the team works together, the bigger the possibilities. Teamwork is only activated by moving from a *me* mindset to a *we* mindset. Having a group of people doesn't mean you have a team. President Woodrow Wilson said, "We should not only use all the brains we have, but all that we can borrow." Teams that work together, win together. Give a brilliant idea to an average team and you will get less. Give an average idea to a brilliant team and you will get more. So goes the team's collective creative ability, so goes what they can produce. The quality of a result comes from the quality of the people creating it. One can't expect to get a fantastic result with a not-so-fantastic team.

> "Teamwork is only activated by moving from a *me* mindset to a *we* mindset."

The team a leader assembles will determine the level of success experienced by all. Your ability to build a world-class inner circle will either make or break your organization.

Here's how you start to create a world-class team:

1) Be Willing To Empower Others

A leader can't truly empower others if they themselves want to hold on to all the power and be the star. A good leader may impress others, but a great leader empowers them. Inspiring leaders are secure enough within themselves to entrust power to those closest to them. When you are able to empower those around you, it creates a culture of true teamwork in your organization. In his book, *Leadership Is Dead: How Influence Is Reviving It*, Jeremie Kubicek wrote, "To empower is a gift of leadership. Accomplishing goals while earning the gratitude of an engaged team creates a lasting legacy of great leadership. The leader who hogs the work and the glory may reap short-term benefits, but over the long term he creates a cynical workforce that is reluctant to follow and ill-prepared to lead."

In order to achieve a higher level of success, you must be ready to entrust power to those you lead. You have to be willing to see others succeed beyond your own success. This may seem like a simple idea, but many leaders struggle when others get more attention than they do. One of the greatest obstacles that block a leader's ability to empower others is ego. The insecurity of losing the spotlight can diminish a leader's ability to delegate to the people around them.

Adolf Hitler interviewed thirty candidates to be his personal chauffeur. His main qualification wasn't based on experience, skill, or personality; it was based on whoever the shortest man was. Infatuated with power and appearance, Hitler wanted to appear tall and muscular in the public spotlight. He wanted others around him short and small in order to build up his own appearance. In fact, the man that Hitler picked to be his chauffeur was so short they literally had to build a special seat for him with blocks under it so he could see the road ahead. Insecure leaders try to make themselves appear better than those around them. Their ego keeps them from truly raising others up. Dwight D. Eisenhower said, "A platoon leader doesn't get his platoon to go by getting up and shouting, 'I am smarter. I am bigger. I am stronger. I am the leader.' He gets them to go along with him because they want to do it for him and they believe in him."

It takes a great deal of humility to be a truly successful leader. Humble leaders achieve more through others because of their ability to let go of arrogant pride. I came across this poem that sums up what it takes to be a humble leader. It's called the *"Indispensable Man"* by Saxon White Kessinger.

> Sometime when you're feeling important;
> Sometime when your ego 's in bloom;
> Sometime when you take it for granted,
> You're the best qualified in the room:
> Sometime when you feel that your going,
> Would leave an unfillable hole,
> Just follow these simple instructions,
> And see how they humble your soul.
> Take a bucket and fill it with water,
> Put your hand in it up to the wrist,
> Pull it out and the hole that's remaining,
> Is a measure of how much you'll be missed.
> You can splash all you wish when you enter,
> You may stir up the water galore,
> But stop, and you'll find that in no time,
> It looks quite the same as before.
> The moral of this quaint example,
> Is to do just the best that you can,
> Be proud of yourself but remember,
> There's no indispensable man.

2) Empower The Right People

Be very selective about who you empower. Better to wait for the right person than to prematurely release the wrong person into a place of authority. Building a team is like building a family; you wouldn't let just anyone come and live with you and be a part of the decision making process in your home. This is a mistake many companies make; they too quickly put bodies into positions without knowing where their heart and skills are. You don't want people just working *for* you; you want them working *with* you. And there is a big difference between someone who works as a hired hand to get tasks done, and someone who works as a committed collaborator to move the company forward. Author Simon Sinek said, "If you hire people just because they can do a job, they'll work for your money. But if you hire people who believe what you believe, they'll work for you with blood and sweat and tears."

> "You don't want people just working *for* you; you want them working *with* you."

There are three things we must do when it comes to getting the right people:

Work With People That Share Your Values

Diversity is a wonderful thing…unless it creates so much tension that it stifles creativity and chemistry. We want to surround ourselves with people who see things differently than we do, but we don't want to have such a gap that we stop working together and start working against each other. Abraham Lincoln's "Team of

Rivals" played along a similar philosophy. He brought in a cabinet of people whose political beliefs ranged from friendly to hostile, so that he had all opinions before him when making a decision. But still, everyone shared the same values, so the "Team of Rivals" worked brilliantly. You must surround yourself with people that have a common value system.

Author Jim Collins teaches that the greatest companies create a cult-like culture around their core ideologies. Everyone has to be working towards the same true north. Even if you disagree on certain ideas, everyone needs to share a collective common bond with each other. In *The Five Dysfunctions of a Team*, Patrick Lencioni wrote, "In the context of building a team, trust is the confidence among the team members that their peers' intentions are good, and that there is no reason to be protective or careful around the group. In essence, teammates must get comfortable being vulnerable with one another." The more comfortable we are with each other, the easier creativity flows.

Work With People That Share Their Life

You want to make sure you connect with people above the level of acquaintance. To be effective, you have to work with a team that shares life together. Relational connection is not a bonus; it's a necessity for success. If work just becomes work, then there is no connection. We must surround ourselves with people that are open and willing to be in community. The more isolated people are, the less creative they will be. Community cultivates collaboration. Don't try to

> "Community cultivates collaboration."

build a team that is only task-oriented and never relationally-oriented. A team that opens up to each other is a team that will open up new doors of opportunity. Some of the greatest times that my teams have excelled have happened after doing getaway retreats together. Getting out of your normal environment gives your team time to dream, plan, and play. These retreats will become some of the most rewarding moments you will experience. It will bring you together in genuine connection, and increase your productivity during day-to-day operations.

Work With People That Share Their Joy

The chemistry must be right in order for teamwork to flow. If the variables are off, the results will be off. No one wants to work in hostile environments where people are angry, upset, frustrated, and rude to each other. These types of environments kill productivity. A beautiful plant can't grow in darkness; neither can creativity grow in negativity. The more negative the environment, the less creative the outcome. Make sure that you work with people that bring you joy, and also bring joy to those they work with. Empowering the wrong person within a team can destroy morale. One toxic mismatch can affect the entire group dynamic.

In their book, *How Full is Your Bucket*, Tom Rath and Donald O. Clifton write, "It is possible for just one or two people to poison an entire workplace. And managers who have tried moving negative people to other departments to alleviate the problem know that 'location, location, location' doesn't apply to these people; they bring their negativity along with them wherever they go. Negative employees can tear through a workplace like a hurricane racing through a coastal town."

3) Trust Their Empowerment

In the nineteenth-century, the greatest tightrope walker in the world was a man named Charles Blondin. On June 30, 1859 he became the first man in history to walk on a tightrope across Niagara Falls. Over twenty-five thousand people gathered to watch him walk 1,100 feet, suspended on a tiny rope, just 160 feet above the raging waters. He worked without a net or even a safety harness of any kind. The slightest slip would have been a fatal one. With all eyes watching him he began to walk out across the chasm. When he safely reached the Canadian side, everyone cheered in relief.

In the days that followed, he walked across the falls again and again. He walked across taking a chair and a stove with him, sat down at the midway point, cooked an omelet, and ate it. Another time, he walked across on stilts, and another time he pushed a wheelbarrow loaded with 350 pounds of cement across the tightrope. One of his most memorable times was when he asked the cheering spectators if they thought he could push a man across in a wheelbarrow. The crowd cheered in agreement. Seeing a man applauding loudly, he asked,

"Sir, do you think I could safely carry you across in this wheelbarrow?"

"Yes, of course," the man replied.

"Get in," the Great Blondin said with a smile.

The man refused.

There was however one man who trusted Blondin, his very own manager, Harry Colcord. Colcord agreed to ride on Blondin, piggyback style, across the tightrope. With 10,000 spectators watching, Colcord climbed on Blondin's back and held on tight as the daredevil walked across Niagara Falls. Colcord had to dismount and remount six times along the way in order for Blondin to rest.

Do you trust your team? Are you willing to get in your team's wheelbarrow and let them take you further?

You have to give authority for others to make decisions, and then allow them to do it. The real test of empowerment is what happens when you are not around. Does your team have the authority and ability to get things done? By not releasing authority you can stall the process of progress. However, when others are trusted to make decisions they will rise to a higher level of ownership in their responsibilities. When leaders give their team authority, it expands productivity. People produce faster when there is minimal red tape to navigate through. One small act of empowerment can change the whole timeline of success.

In fact, numerous studies published in the *Journal of Personality and Social Psychology* have been conducted about the effects of perceived power. The following were a series of experiments done...

> In Experiment 1, participants who possessed structural power in a group task were more likely to take a card in a simulated game of blackjack than those who lacked power. In Experiment 2, participants primed with high power were more likely to act against an annoying stimulus (a fan) in the environment, suggesting that the experience of power leads to the performance of goal-directed behavior. In Experiment 3, priming high power led to action in a social dilemma regardless of whether that action had prosocial or antisocial consequences.

The conclusions all returned the same; people who feel powerful are more proactive in their behavior. Giving power to those you lead greatly enhances their potential to act. But you cannot give power and then usurp them every time they try to exercise it. Your team must learn to fly on their own. A mother eagle understands empowerment. She stirs up her nest to make it uncomfortable for her little eaglets. Her purpose is to get the eaglets out of their safe zone so that they can learn to fly. We, like the mother eagle, need to help stir the comfortable nests of those we lead. We need to give them authority to move on to greater things. By doing this, we help others develop their potential.

Never stand alone. Leadership is not a lonely place when you are doing it right.

Q*uestions To Think About:*

A) What areas are you holding on to that need to be delegated?

_____

_____

_____

B) How can you start to create more teamwork with those around you?

_____

_____

_____

C) If you were to expand your team and bring on new people, what two to three skills would you need from the new team members that joined?

1._____

_____

2._____

_____

3._____

_____

Leadology Challenge:

Every great leader has a great inner circle. A group of people they change the world with. You are only as good as those you surround yourself with. To be a great leader, you have to be a great team-builder. As my mentor Dr. John C. Maxwell teaches, one is too small a number to achieve greatness. Who is your inner circle? If you can't answer that quickly, you probably don't have an inner circle. You need to purposefully know who they are and what they bring to the table. The first job of any leader is to develop key leaders they can count on by releasing authority and responsibility to them.

Make a list of your inner circle. Think of how you are going to help take them to the next level. Begin to make a list of what you are going to start handing off to each one of them. Prioritize the next projects, tasks, decisions, and so on…that you are going to release. Make sure you are spending the most time with this group by giving them your very best. Too many leaders give themselves to the wrong people, and then only have a small portion left to give to the right people. Change that by being proactive about spending your best time with your team. Author Jim Rohn said, "You are the average of the five people you spend the most time with." Make sure your inner circle is the right one.

THE
CABIN
PRESSURE

|| Idea #6 ||

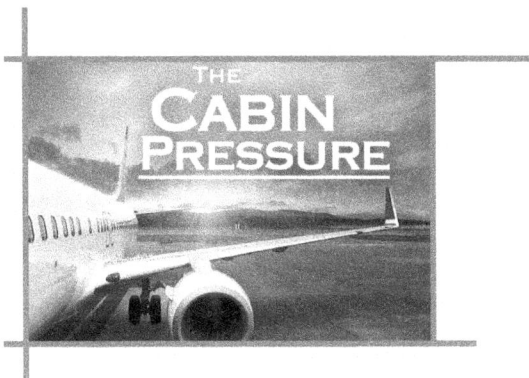

The Cabin Pressure

The higher you go, the more pressure there is to perform. Always ascending and never stabilizing eventually causes burnout. Leaders must practice the art of balancing the stress of success and the renewal of rest.

I'll never forget my very first time flying in an airplane. I was a young teenager going to meet up with my parents in Arizona, where they were vacationing. I was a little nervous since I didn't know what to expect. The thought of being…who knows how high up in the air, strapped into a chair with only a few inches of metal surrounding me, seemed a bit nerve-racking to say the least. But I was courageous enough to take on the challenge. A friend dropped me off at the airport, and trying to keep my cool, I waved and thanked him for the ride.

At first, things went smoothly. I made it through all of the airport checkpoints without a hitch, and it was no time before I was at my gate. Not long after I arrived, I heard the gate clerk's signal telling me it was time for my row to board. This flying thing was a piece of cake so far. What was I so worked up about? It was when I entered the plane that things began to change. I quickly noticed how cramped the cabin was. Shouldn't there be more room inside such a huge jet? Still, I was doing O.K. I located my seat and was able to get my luggage stored properly, my seat in the upright position, my safety belt snuggly fastened, and all exits located and stored in my memory banks. The engines began to roar as the jet backed away from the airport terminal and headed for the runway. No big deal.

Then we came to a complete stop, and what I thought was a roar just moments ago sounded like a purr compared to the sound blasting out of the jet now. The whole cabin started to shake and suddenly we picked up speed. I felt myself being pushed against the back of my seat as we began to takeoff and ascend into the air. We hit some turbulence on the way up. The feeling of my stomach dropping as we bounced up and down was extremely unsettling to me. I wasn't sure if this was supposed to be happening. I tried to look normal but I couldn't help but think that a wing was going to rip off of the plane at any moment or maybe an engine was going to fly off into the great blue yonder.

At this point, the real trouble began. Something terrible that I couldn't explain began to happen to me. It scared me to death…literally. I had no doubt in my mind that I was about to die! As we continued our ascension, my right ear started to clog up and a pressure like I had never felt before started to build up in my head. I had felt a similar sensation before while driving in the mountains. But this? This was something massively worse.

I remembered my parents telling me to yawn in order to release the tension on our drives in the mountains, and not knowing what else to do, I, as calmly as I could, began to try to make myself yawn. Not wanting to draw attention to myself and let the whole world see my panic, I began to nonchalantly yawn and open my mouth wide, but nothing was changing. In fact, the pressure just kept building and building. My nervousness really started to get the best of me at this point, especially when the right side of my head started twitching uncontrollably from the pain. My whole head began to shake and I felt like my eyeball was going to pop out of its socket and go sailing to the front of the plane. As this vision passed through my mind, I began to frantically pray that it wouldn't come true. I had now reached the point of not caring about my coolness factor. I didn't care who saw my panic. I needed to fix this problem fast or I was going to have to invest in an eye-patch and start calling people mayte.

I began yawning with my mouth as wide as it would go. I was twisting, tugging, and pulling on my ears, as I grabbed my head in pain. To make matters worse, my neck started to tighten up from all the pressure, which caused me to tilt my head over into my neighbor's "personal space." My neck completely stiffened up and I couldn't move it back to its normal position. My neighbor looked as scared as I did. I am not sure he knew how to handle my frantic display of fear. I thought I had met my end, not because the plane was going down from the frightening turbulence, or because one of the engines was going to detach from the plane, but because my head was going to explode all over the place.

Luckily, at just about the point when I was going to burst, my ear popped and the pressure was released. I think it blew my neighbor's hair out of place when it blasted out the side of my head. It was one of the craziest feelings I have ever felt. I let out an extremely loud sigh of relief and then noticed everyone looking at me with horror and worry. It was just like a scene from a movie; however, I definitely was not the hero.

I learned a valuable lesson that day; the higher you go the more pressure you'll face. For every new level, there is a new devil you have to fight. In fact, the more successful you become, the greater the pressure to perform will be as you battle the forces of imbalance. Leaders are driven to move forward and ascend, but they must learn how to decompress from time to time. You can't always be in overdrive or your emotional engine will overheat and stall from destabilization. As you climb the ladder of growth, you have to master the art of recovery, or you'll internally combust under the pressure. I once served under a very fast-paced, high-energy leader that only knew one speed…Mach3! He became very frustrated at anyone who didn't move at his pace. One day my leader's mentor came to visit our team to do some training. After the meeting, I made a quick light-hearted comment to him about how intense it was serving under my boss/his protégé.

He then looked at me and said, "Yeah, he'll learn one day. You can't live life as a full-on sprint all the time. You have to pace yourself for the long haul." His truth became a fulfilling prophecy when years later my leader had to step out of his role because his life had unraveled under the pressure he put on himself.

Life has to be lived as a marathon, not a short dash. There is a huge difference between working hard and harmfully working. Leaders must set a realistic pace in order to set

> "The greater the cause we are working toward, the more temptation there is to lose ourselves in it."

themselves up for longevity. There is a temptation to exert so much energy into what we do that it consumes our life. In fact, the greater the cause we are working toward, the more temptation there is to lose ourselves in it. But great leaders know how to work hard in bursts, then replenish their energy with rest.

In *The Making Of A Corporate Athlete,* Jim Loehr and Tony Schwartz explained how they spent years training and developing Olympic athletes in performance management. This led them to the corporate world to train world-class leaders in productivity with the same principles they taught athletes. They made a significant impact on the productivity of many organizations by enhancing employee performance. They wrote this about the importance of balance:

> "In a corporate environment that is changing at warp speed, performing consistently at high levels is more difficult and more necessary than ever. Narrow interventions simply aren't sufficient anymore. Compa-

nies can't afford to address their employees' cognitive capacities while ignoring their physical, emotional, and spiritual well being. On the playing field or in the boardroom, high performance depends as much on how people renew and recover energy as on how they expend it, on how they manage their lives as much as on how they manage their work. When people feel strong and resilient—physically, mentally, emotionally, and spiritually—they perform better, with more passion, for longer. They win, their families win, and the corporations that employ them win."

According to their research and real life applications, the whole key to performance rests on the ability to renew and recover from stress. The rhythm of productivity hinges not just on what you do, but also on what you don't do. Taking time to refresh enhances the times when you are working. This is seen in every aspect of life. There is a very effective form of physical exercise called high-intensity interval training. This training is based on the science that our bodies are designed to function more optimally when they are subject to short bursts of energy and then moments of recovery. Not only does this apply to our physical bodies, but it also applies to our emotional and mental capacity as well.

Almost every religion teaches about the importance of rest and renewal. In the Bible, God commanded a Sabbath rest for His people. This Sabbath was about creating a rhythm for releasing potential. The Jews were enslaved by the Egyptians to work with brick and mortar every day from sun up till sun down. They built Egypt's structures with their bare hands. Their identity slowly shifted from worshippers to workers after each generation passed. Their self-worth was determined by how many bricks they could lay in a day. Those who couldn't reach the quota were beaten, and at times even killed if they didn't produce.

So God sent a leader, Moses, to deliver them from the oppression. Later, God created the Sabbath - a day of rest - so they could find their true selves and understand their value was not in what they did, but in Who's they were. To this day, the Jews, and Christians alike, still practice this tradition. Rabbi Abraham Joshua Heschel said, "Sabbath gives the world the spiritual energy it needs to exist for another six days."

Every leader has to keep the rhythm of work, renew, work, renew, work, renew, work, renew, etc... or else their productivity will eventually fade away.

So how do we decompress?

1) Know When To Say No

Do you remember the national drug campaign that Nancy Reagan started in the 1980s? The slogan was "Just Say No!" The advertisement focused on the importance of saying "No" to peer pressure in the context of illegal drugs. The phrase "Just Say No" first emerged when Nancy Reagan was visiting Longfellow Elementary School in Oakland, California and was asked by a schoolgirl what to do if she was offered drugs. The first lady responded by saying, "Just say no."

"Just Say No" is more than an illegal drug campaign, though; every leader on the planet should also adopt it when it comes to their schedule and the use of their time. If you don't know how to say "No" you'll never be able to say "Yes" to the best. For everything you add to your schedule there should be something you are giving up which is of lesser value. If you are only adding to your responsibilities, you will eventually collapse from the weight of too much baggage. Only adding but never subtracting from your schedule slowly evolves you into a time hoarder. Eventually, you will become unproductively consumed with the "busyness" of a cluttered life. You will be overwhelmed with the chaos of your responsibilities. You'll become increasingly less effective if your schedule gets too cluttered.

> "For everything you add to your schedule there should be something you are giving up which is of lesser value."

Most people are saying "Yes" to the things they shouldn't be doing and "No" to the things they should be doing. Even when we say "Yes" to the things that are good, that means we are saying "No" to the things that are best for us. Don't get lost in the good zone; get going in the best zone by learning the power of knowing the word "No." Only give yourself to the things that matter most and bring the most return.

Sometimes by doing less, we do more.

2) Know When To Get Away

Howard Tinsley, PhD, an emeritus professor of psychology with Southern Illinois University, has studied the benefits of leisure since the 1970s. His immense research has taught us that vacationing releases two critical neurotransmitters: dopamine and serotonin. These "happy" neurotransmitters have the ability to increase focus, motivation, self-worth, enjoyment, and a host of other positive enhancers. Research has found that workers who take more vacation time consistently receive better scores on their end-of-the-year performance reviews.

The effect isn't small, either; the boost is nearly a 10% increase! Compared to workers who didn't take time off, the vacationers also tend to be happier with their jobs and stick around long-term. Americans work more hours and take less vacation than nearly 98% of other countries in the world. No wonder so many employees are stressed out and waning in their effectiveness.

If you aren't taking time to get away, let me tell you bluntly, "Get Out!" That's right. Get out of the office, the projects, the tasks, and go somewhere that will refresh you. And no, I am not just talking about going home or to your local hot spot; I am also talking about getting away to somewhere new that is detached from familiarity. Each year I have made it a habit to rent a cabin for a few nights all by myself to refresh and gain clarity from the busyness of my schedule and responsibilities. It was hard at first to leave my wife and two daughters to get away alone. But the payoff has been incredible. I now look forward to my retreat each year because it rejuvenates me and allows me to gain perspective.

Every few months we should be getting away even if it is for a night. You may not "feel like you need it," but don't wait to "feel like you need it" or it will be harder to refresh, and it will take much longer than a short trip to recover. The reason you "feel like you need it" is because you've waited too long to do it.

Be proactive about refreshing your energy by systematically getting away.

3) Know You Need Hobbies

If you did a study on some of the most successful people, you would find several common denominators among them. One of the denominators is that they all have hobbies they are passionate about. For example:

- Former President, George W. Bush, is an avid painter
- Actress Susan Sarandon calls herself a ping-pong propagandist
- Billionaire Richard Branson's favorite sport is kite boarding
- Investor Warren Buffet plays a lot of online bridge
- Inventor Albert Einstein loved to sail
- Apple Founder Steve Jobs played guitar
- Actress Angelina Jolie collects daggers
- Google Co-Founder Sergey Brin does trapeze

Hobbies allow us to escape from work and replenish our quality of life. All work plus no play equals psychological disarray. When we find enjoyable hobbies, we are in essence investing into our well being. Having healthy outlets allows us to decompress from stress. Everyone should have a hobby that they are able to get lost in at times. This oscillation from working to playing generates creative energy. Remember playing cars as a kid with hot wheels, micromachines, or whatever type of

> "All work plus no play equals psychological disarray."

toy you had? You could set up tracks with three-hundred-sixty-degree loops right in the middle.

These loops would create momentum for the car to keep going until it reached the finish line. As soon as the car made its way down the loop, it would pick up an extreme amount of force to keep moving. In the same way, hobbies create a propelling loop that gives us the mental and physical strength to keep persevering. They reward us with improved creativity, emotional recharging, self-confidence, stress relief, social connection, idea generating, leadership lessons, and broader awareness. Simply put…hobbies are extremely good for your mind. Tons of world changing ideas and solutions have been conceived during recreation. For instance, 3M inventor Art Fry had his breakthrough moment while on the companies private golf course where he got the idea for post-it-notes. George de Mestral was on a hunting trip when he noticed burdock burs sticking to his clothes and his dog's fur. Curiosity led him to study the burs to figure out why they stuck so well and he used what he learned to create Velcro.

Ideas come to us more frequently when we are in a good state of mind. The word *recreation* means "to create again or renew." Recreation always precedes creation. When you are fresh you are at your best. Make sure you are investing time into your leisure so that life becomes a holistic journey. And don't just *have* a hobby, but make sure you are consistently *doing* your hobby. Author James A. Michener said, "The master in the art of living makes little distinction between his work and his play, his labor and his leisure, his mind and his body, his information and his recreation, his love and his religion. He hardly knows which is which. He simply pursues his vision of excellence at whatever he does, leaving others to decide whether he is working or playing. To him he's always doing both." To be an effective leader, embrace work and recovery as equally important responsibilities.

Q*uestions To Think About:*

A) On a scale of 1-10 how is your rhythm of life currently?

Rhythm   1 2 3 4 5 6 7 8 9 10

Why did you rate it like this?

_____

_____

_____

B) Why do you think leisure time is important to productivity?

_____

_____

_____

C) What three things that rejuvenate your energy and focus?

1._____

_____

2._____

_____

3._____

_____

Leadology Challenge:

Most people only get around to hobbies and leisure time when they happen to have some left over. However, highly successful people schedule it in just as they would an important meeting with a client. You will never rest and recover if you wait until everything is done to do it. You must be proactive about creating sacred time for yourself.

I want you to first make a list of the things that you enjoy doing. You can't know what to do with your leisure time if you don't know what you want to be doing. Many people find themselves lost when they have some unaccounted time because they don't have a plan for what to do. Thus, they sit around thinking about what to do and consequently waste their time and end up never really doing anything of value. Have a list of things that you enjoy doing so you can go to it whenever you allocate time.

The next step is to proactively schedule your recovery time in before others beat you to the punch. If you already have sacred time blocked out on your calendar, you can have a genuine reason to say, "No," to everyone's request. You need to create rhythm with your schedule, so make sure you are intentionally keeping it in the oscillation of work time, then recovery time. The quality of life is more important than the quantity of it. Maximize your life by creating a cadence of productivity.

The Conference Dinner

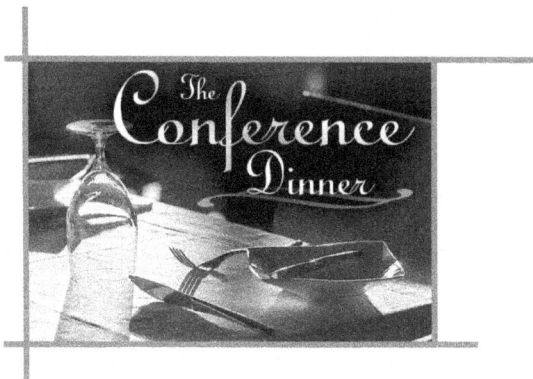

The Conference Dinner

Feeling overwhelmed by your dreams and underwhelmed by your ability to reach them is a wonderful place to be. Great leaders are willing to go to where they've never been in order to get to where they want to go.

In my early twenties, I was invited to teach leadership development to a group of teenagers at a huge conference in Nashville, Tennessee. This wasn't just any group of teenagers though; this group happened to be comprised of the sons and daughters of a large MLM (Multi-Level-Marketing) business group that had over six hundred team members. The business group was holding their annual weekend blowout conference at a prestigious hotel and conference center. A friend and I were tasked with taking the hundred and fifty or so teenage children of these business leaders and teaching them leadership and success principles while their parents attended the conference all day.

A gorgeous banquet room was reserved for us, and we had the creative freedom to shape the whole experience as we saw fit. The truth was, this was the first major leadership conference I had ever had the privilege to speak at and help lead. And the even bigger truth was that I was in way over my head, and I knew it. These truths became even more evident at the main kick-off dinner on the night before the training began. Since we were the honored guests for the weekend, a table had been reserved for us directly up front, by the stage, in the huge banquet hall. The whole room was assigned seating based on the success each individual had acquired over the last business year. So it's important to understand that my friend and I were sitting at the table with the head honchos of the entire group. We're talking about team members who are triple multi-millionaire, double-platinum, emerald-honored, and whatever other title you can think of.

The event kicked off with high energy. People were shouting and dancing and showing their excitement that the long-awaited conference was finally starting. My friend and I waited to be announced before we entered. When our names were called, we walked from the back of the room to our specially designated table, located front and center. People were staring and pointing at us as though we were royalty. They had no idea we hadn't won this coveted seat by being top sellers. As dinner began, so did conversation.

The person next to me began talking about his 5th home that he had just purchased in yet another country: Italy, this time. He shared stories of success: two-hundred-million-dollar sales closed just days ago, among others. I remember that throughout the course of the meal, my friend and I kept looking at each other in amazement as we took stock of our current level of financial stability. In fact, while pondering my financial situation, I realized I had overdrawn my bank account earlier in the day when I purchased a candy bar. That was the most expensive candy bar I had ever purchased; it had cost me almost twenty dollars, ultimately.

So during a quiet moment, in between talks of Tuscany and millions of dollars, I quietly leaned over to my friend and told him that I might have to borrow some money to get me through the weekend. The funny thing was, he told me that due to his place of employment not being able to cut him a check for the last few weeks, he didn't have much money either. Yep...we were way out of our league. But even though we felt out of place, the teen training went phenomenally well and we were able to make a significant impact in those teenagers' lives. That weekend I learned that even though we may feel overwhelmed, we have to step out from our fears and step into our potential.

Feeling like being in way over your head, just as I did at the conference, is exactly the place you should strive to be. It is said that when you get to a point where you're in over your head, it doesn't really matter how much deeper you go; you're still in over your head, so you might as well just keep diving in! Feeling overwhelmed by your potential and underwhelmed by your ability to succeed can discourage you or drive you forward.

The issue lies in how you respond. If you let discouragement set in, you will give up in your pursuit for more. But if you allow discipline to motivate you, it can cause you to pursue greater possibilities. Extraordinary leaders are willing to step out even when the tasks ahead seem insurmountable. They understand that true growth takes place outside of the comfort zone. The next level of success for you and your team does not lie within what you have accomplished; it lies within what you haven't accomplished yet. You will never be more than you are now, unless you do something you've never done. All great advancements were a result of someone attempting something that was beyond what was comfortable. In fact, most exploration of new ideas comes with a cost. That cost is abandoning your limiting fear. If your dreams don't scare you, you're not dreaming big enough.

> "If your dreams don't scare you, you're not dreaming big enough."

Humans are like turtles; sometimes you have to stick your neck out to move forward.

Fear is the greatest enemy of progress. It is the arch-villain of greatness. It prevents us from experiencing the potential we have within us and the possibilities of achievement around us. Not long ago, my family and I went to a local water park for a getaway. We decided to go on a weekday, so we would have the best chance of having the water park all to ourselves. Our plan worked. We went down the lazy river, played in the faucets, and swam around in the pools without waiting in lines or having to make our way through the crowds.

It was amazing. The whole time we were enjoying the attractions, my youngest daughter was eyeing the "big slide." She watched her sister and me go down the slide over and over and over. I kept asking if she wanted to try it, but she was too scared. However, after some time, she built up enough courage to attempt this daring feat. I took her hand and began the long journey to the top of the slide. She looked down after each giant step we took up the stairs to see how high we were. Her anticipation was growing. When we got to the top, she took a deep breath, looked at me, and then plunged down the slide.

After we both made it to the bottom, she looked me in the eye, her face alight with joy, and squealed, "What have I been missing! Can we go again, Daddy?" On our way up the second time, I asked her if she had been really scared the first time we went down. With wide eyes, she answered me with an emphatic, "YES!" Then with the assumption she had overcome her fear, I said, "But now you aren't scared anymore, are you?" Her reply caught me off guard. She said, "No, I am still scared, but I'm going down anyway!"

When courage resides in your heart, you're bolder, stronger, and more effective in all you do. Your bravery will push you to overcome any obstacles standing in the way. Courage conquers fear and pushes you to do things you never thought possible. It drives you to move beyond your comfort zones and accomplish greater things. Courage is the fuel for a success-filled life.

Most people are unaware of the courage they already possess. This potential rests inside them, but they live in self-doubt, fear, and unbelief. Understand that courage is not the absence of fear; rather, courage is moving ahead in spite of fear. And in order to live with a limitless faith in yourself, you must face your fears, head on, without compromise.

There are three main fears that every leader must battle:

1) Fear Of The Unknown

One of the scariest feelings that can overtake us is fear of the unknown. Our minds tend to imagine the worst when we do not know what lies ahead in our future. When I continued to ask my daughter to go down the big slide, she didn't know what to expect, therefore she feared the worst and it kept her from stepping out. Fear is a pessimist; it has no hope. When fear of the unknown comes upon us, it turns our minds into a wonderland of uncertainty and insecurity. When uncertainty and insecurity grow within, they start to control our decision-making.

It would be extraordinary to know about everything in life before it happened, but life doesn't allow us that luxury. While my seventeen-year-old nephew was thinking about who he was going to ask to the prom, a pretty girl approached him at school and said, "Hey, if you were to ask me to prom, I wouldn't say no."

The rest is history.

Wouldn't life be great if we knew the outcome before we had to step out and take a risk? Even though 20/20 foresight would be infinitely better than 20/20 hindsight, we do not have to live under the control of fear. Envision a life without fear of the unknown. Imagine being free to trust that whatever you do, you know you'll have the ability to achieve it. This is the faith it takes to live without limits. We do not have to fear the unknown. Ralph Waldo Emerson said, "He who is not everyday conquering some fear has not learned the secret of life."

Never let your fear of the unknown keep you from having faith in the unseen. If we spend all of our time thinking about what could go wrong,

> "Never let your fear of the unknown keep you from having faith in the unseen."

we will miss the possibilities of seeing what could go right. The truth is that fear and worry exaggerate themselves to the point we feel overcome by them. We can either feel overwhelmed by what lies ahead of us, or we can choose to live a life of overcoming what lies ahead of us. The bald eagle powerfully illustrates what it means to soar above and beyond the limits of the unknown. While other birds fly away from violent, windy conditions, the eagle meets the raging tempest head-on. Eagles fly into a storm, harness the power of the strong winds, and use this power to propel them above the turbulence and danger. We have to develop ourselves to be like an eagle when it comes to overcoming our fear of the unknown conditions around us. We must challenge ourselves to look beyond our limits and see higher ground, just as the eagle does.

2) Fear Of Others

Too often we allow what people think about us to determine our level of courage. When we fear what others say about us, we become trapped in a prison of self-consciousness. In *The Life of Andrew Jackson*, Marquis James tells of a Sunday morning in 1818 when Circuit Preacher Peter Cartwright delivered a sermon. The traveling preacher was warned that the up-and-coming president, General Andrew Jackson, would be in attendance, and that he needed to keep his remarks inoffensive, as to not upset the general. After all, Andrew Jackson was well known for his fiery temper and deadly duels. However, during his message, Peter Cartwright came out and said, "I have been told that Andrew Jackson is here today and to hold back any offensive remarks. What I must say is that Andrew Jackson will go to hell if he does not repent of his sin." It is said that after the sermon, the general approached Cartwright and said, "If I had a regiment of men like you, I could whip the world."

What we perceive in our mind is what we project around us. Our thoughts create the lens through which we view the world. That is why beauty is truly in the eye of the beholder. If someone constantly thinks they are unlikable, then every interaction with others will be seen through that lens. They will feel disliked by just about everyone they come in contact with. However, if someone has thoughts of peace towards others, no matter what happens, they will tend to live in harmony with others.

One of my favorite authors, James Allen, shared this great idea: "To live continually in thoughts of ill will, cynicism, suspicion, and envy, is to be confined in a self-made prison hole. But to think well of all, to be cheerful with all, to patiently learn to find the good in all—such unselfish thoughts are the very portals of heaven; and to dwell day by day in thoughts of peace toward every creature will bring abounding peace to their possessor."

Never let the fear of others keep you from stepping out in bold courageous faith. Envision having no fear of rejection. Imagine not being afraid of what others think or say about you in regard to your courage. Picture all you could do if you were free from the worry of what might happen to your reputation. Remember this: What you fear about others will only limit the difference you can make in them.

Don't forsake what you know must be done out of a fear of what others will think about you.

3) Fear Of Failure

Don't ever wait for circumstances to be perfect before courageously stepping out into greater opportunities. Too many people want to wait for their fear to disappear before they take a leap of faith; but faith does not operate that way. Courage is about stepping out even when you are unsure of the outcome. Those who wait until they feel ready are usually just living with an excuse for their apprehension. Though my daughter was scared to experience the waterslide, she still went down.

You and I have to step out in unwavering bravery despite our fears. If I were to ask you to walk across an 8-foot beam that was only 2 feet off the ground, would you do it? Probably so. You probably wouldn't think twice about it. However, if I were to raise it 5 feet off the ground, would you still do it? Maybe. What if I raised it 25 feet off the ground? What about 50 feet? What about 500 feet? What about 5,000 feet? At what point did you drop out? Why did you drop out? Was it because you do not know how to walk across an 8-foot beam? Of course not. It takes the exact same skill to walk across an 8-foot beam at 500 feet off the ground as it does to walk across an 8-foot beam at 2 feet off the ground. Nothing changed in terms of your ability to make it across. What changed is your fear. Fear keeps us from going higher and reaching for greater opportunities.

Your sight may scare you; it can put fear in your mind. The reality is: If you knew the beam was no higher than 2 feet off the ground, you would have very little fear in crossing it. You're only afraid because of what you see. You're afraid of falling. The fear of failure can cause you to stop pressing on in your courage. Disappointments will be a part of life, but they are not forever. Every one of us will fail at some point, sooner or later. Even the best of the best have had their share of setbacks. Think about these household names who did not start off as the successes that we know them to be...

- Babe Ruth, who had the record for most home runs, also had the record for most strikeouts.
- Michael Jordan was cut from his high school basketball team.
- Walt Disney went bankrupt seven times. A newspaper editor fired him because, "He lacked imagination and had no good ideas."
- Henry Ford forgot to put reverse in his first automobile, but it

didn't stop him from building cars.

- Star Wars received this review from a movie critic: "Dull new world, as exciting as last year's weather report."
- The artist, Van Gogh, sold one painting in his lifetime.
- Steven Spielberg dropped out of high school. He applied to attend film school three times but was unsuccessful because of his C grade average.
- Twenty-seven different publishers rejected Dr. Seuss' first book, *To Think That I Saw It on Mulberry Street.*
- Many record labels rejected the Beatles. In a famous rejection, Decca Records said, "Guitar groups are on the way out," and "The Beatles have no future in show business."

Always remember: Failure is not forever; it's just a moment to learn. Henry Ford said, "Failure is simply the opportunity to begin again, this time more intelligently." When we stop moving forward for fear of having a bad experience, we waste the possibility of having a great experience. The key to overcoming failure is to keep our eyes forward. Everyone has faced, is facing, or will face failures in their life. The question is not, "Will I ever fail?"

> "Every failure brings with it a seed of success, but we must extract the growth lessons from our failures in order to learn from them."

The question is, "How will I respond to failure?" Every failure brings with it a seed of success, but we must extract the growth lessons from our failures in order to learn from them. If you allow failure to keep you down, you will miss out on great opportunities. Motivational speaker, Les Brown, put it this way: "When life knocks you down, try to land on your back. Because if you can look up, you can get up." Leaders get back up from failure and keep on keepin' on. Building upon failure is how we reach high enough to become successful in what we do. Thomas J. Watson, the former chairman and CEO of IBM said, "If you want to succeed, double your failure rate."

Q*uestions To Think About:*

A) Rate which fear you struggle with the most. Mark 1 for the most common and 3 being the least.

Fear of the Unknown   **Fear of Others**   **Fear of Failure**

_____   _____   _____

B) Why is being "in over your head" a good place to be?

_____

_____

_____

C) List three areas you want to start challenging yourself to step out further in.

1._____

_____

2._____

_____

3._____

_____

*L*eadology Challenge:

I've always liked the scene on the hit TV show, The Office, in which manager Michael Scott, played by Steve Carell, talks about his strengths and weaknesses. In an episode from Season 3, Michael Scott is invited to interview for a position at Dunder Mifflin corporate headquarters. During the interview with David Wallace, Dunder Mifflin's CEO, the following conversation takes place:

> **David Wallace:** So, let me ask you a question right off the bat. What do you think are your greatest strengths as a manager?
> **Michael Scott:** Why don't I tell you what my greatest weaknesses are? I work too hard. I care too much. And sometimes I can be too invested in my job.
> **David:** Okay. And your strengths?
> **Michael:** Well, my weaknesses are actually...strengths.
> **David:** Oh. Yes. Very good.
> **Michael:** Thank you.

Saying you don't have any fears is like saying you don't have any weaknesses. We need to be truthful about the fears we face and understand how to break through them. The truth is we all face fears of various kinds that can limit our decision making and risk taking. Begin to overcome your fears by taking practical steps to face them. Make a plan to push yourself further from whatever it is that may be holding you back from being coura-geous. If there is a conversation you are avoiding, make a plan to talk to that person. If there is a dream in your heart to accomplish a goal, make a plan to start working toward it. If you have a fear of failing at a certain task, start to step out and try it anyway. The more you face your fears, the easier it becomes to be courageous.

THE TARANTULA HAIR

The Tarantula Hair

Leaders have to deal with sensitive, hard people problems. It is in these difficult moments that the leader's strength and resolve is exposed. Challenging times can either be an obstacle to an organization, or an opportunity to do what's right and move forward.

Years ago, I was part of my church's leadership team that took over twenty high school and college-aged students on a mission trip to Central America. We went to Belize for a few days and then made our way up into Mexico, sharing hope and offering help to those in need. It was an incredible experience for all of us. But at times, this trip felt a little like an Indiana Jones type adventure.

Let me explain.

After months of planning and preparing for our trip, our plane finally touched down on foreign soil. We left the airport on an old, beaten-up bus that looked and smelled like it had hauled its fair share of chickens and pigs around the countryside. After winding through miles of roadway—deeper into the rainforest jungle and further away from civilization—we arrived at our destination: a lodge where we would be stationed for the remainder of our stay in Belize. As we exited the bus and started to head to our rooms, we realized that there was something different about this lodge.

On further inspection, we noticed that there were no windows, no doors, and no bathrooms in the facility. When we asked about the bathroom situation, our host handed us a shovel and told us to go dig some holes in the brush away from the lodge. You can imagine that after a long flight followed by a lengthy trip on bumpy jungle roads, our first priority was rounding up some young guys from our group and having them start digging holes at lightning speed.

After taking care of business, the reality of our situation began to settle in. Here we were, a leadership team in charge of twenty plus students, in the middle of who knows where, preparing to make camp in what appeared to be the shell of what may have once been a type of building. Concerned by this, we asked our host if it was safe to stay here given there were no windows or doors to keep things on the outside out, and things on the inside in. We were assured that everything was perfectly safe...well...except for the fruit bats that may fly in at night while we were sleeping. But we were told not to worry because they were harmless and wouldn't bother anyone. It was mentioned, though, that we should sleep completely covered by our sleeping bags...just in case. And it was also recommended that all females sleep on the lower level of the lodge since they may not be "used to the bats." I guess as guys, we should have somehow been "used to them."

But as our stay in Belize came to a close, we could honestly say that all went well. We made it through our stay, safe and sound. Little did we know that these accommodations would be considered the five-star Hilton of our trip before it was all over. It was now time for us to say goodbye to Belize and head to Mexico. We would be staying in a hotel in the middle of a city and we were ready to get back to civilization.

If only we knew that the scariest part of our trip was about to happen.

Pulling in to the hotel parking lot, our expectations were high. We were dreaming of bat-free nights, being surrounded by the comforts of glass-paneled windows, and being tucked snugly in our hotel rooms behind doors, complete with knobs and hinges. The idea of using a bathroom without the fear of something taking a bite out of places that it just shouldn't brought smiles to our faces. But as we stepped off the bus, our hopes came crashing down.

When we entered the building, we figured that, by our best guess, this hotel would be ranked a negative four-star on a good day. It came packed with every creepy crawly creature you could think of. This insect infestation made us wish for our bat friends that we had taken for granted in Belize. There was less wildlife in the rainforest jungle than there was in this one hotel. Words don't even do justice to how dilapidated this place was. The facilities were so bad that half of our team preferred sleeping on the stinky, smelly bus/animal cargo hauler overnight. The next morning as we started preparing for our day, things got really interesting, really quickly.

It wasn't long after we awoke that we heard something that would make any leader's heart stop: one of girls that was under our care screaming at the top of her lungs. Was she being attacked? Did the roof fall in on her? Was she being eaten by a giant lizard that crawled up through the toilet? A few leaders and I ran across the courtyard as fast as we could in an attempt to rescue her. When we reached this young lady in distress, what we saw baffled us. She was flailing around, screaming, and pulling at her super long, super curly head of hair. Had the horror of the night in this roach motel driven her mad? In an effort to figure out why she was so frantic, we tried to get her to calm down and explain to us what was happening, but she just kept screaming gibberish and running around in circles. We were finally able to decipher some of the gibberish and realized she was shouting, "There's something in my hair!"

After some coaxing, we got her to calm down enough to try to start removing this unwelcome "something" from her thick, curly locks. As we dug through her jungle of hair, we soon targeted the culprit. It turned out to be a gigantic, hairy, long-legged, Mexican tarantula tangled up and trying to get free. It looked just as intent on getting free from the girl as the girl was of getting free from it. Knowing this young woman was already frightened out of her mind, we, as a leadership team, decided to hide from her what we had found. We told her to just sit still and we would get the "bug" untangled in no time. No time took a little longer than expected. That tarantula was really tangled up in there, and none of us really wanted to just reach in there and grab it.

But finally, after digging through her curls with some sticks we had found laying nearby, we were able to pry the little beast out of her hair. I will never forget that…and I know the young girl will never…ever…forget it. In fact, I'm not sure she slept at all for the rest of the trip.

Like the situations we faced in Central America, every leader will deal with unforeseen challenges, conflicts, and crisis. Situations occur that are unpleasant and sometimes downright terrible for everyone. Tarantula-type attitudes, behaviors, and disagreements can cause unsettling work environments. Just like we had to calm the young girl down before we could remove the tarantula, we as leaders have to figure out healthy ways to untangle conflict and crisis with and among the people we lead. It is in these moments that real leaders step up to the plate and deal with the issues at hand. Martin Luther King Jr. said, "The ultimate measure of a man is not where he stands in moments of comfort and convenience, but where he stands at times of challenge and controversy."

No one is immune to conflict. Even the best of organizations deal with difficult challenges. But conflict, or even crisis, isn't what will make or break your organization. It's how you handle these challenges that will determine if you succeed. Problems are not problems unless you don't do anything with the problem, then it really becomes a problem.

It is interesting to note the word *crisis* comes from the Greek word *krisis*, meaning a turning point of decision. You see, every crisis brings with it an opportunity to respond for the better or for the worse. The result is determined by your response. Trouble is inevitable; misery is optional. It's not just what you go through that makes the difference; it's how you go through it.

Here are the do's and don'ts of effectively dealing with challenges:

1) Don't Avoid Confrontation

Confrontation is never enjoyable. No matter what personality type a leader possesses, they have to learn how to be candid and honest with their team. Trust is lost on the grounds of shady, shy, intimidated leadership. I admit candor has been a struggle for me as a leader because of my desire to please everyone. I am not a confrontational type of individual. It makes me uncomfortable and nervous when extreme tension arises. I thrive off of inspiration and positivity, so, for many years, I avoided being candid with team members. It cost me many mistakes and caused some heartache early on. I avoided removing people from positions that weren't the right fit, and I didn't hold people accountable for their actions. But I began to realize that if I was going to truly help others, I needed to be more upfront and honest with them.

I have found that the longer you wait to deal with situations, the more awkward it becomes to confront them. The time frame in which you confront issues determines, to a great extent, the outcome. If everyone around you is waiting for you to take action on a specific issue, it's likely time for you to do something. The longer you wait to act the more respect and influence you will lose with your superiors, your peers, and those you are leading.

> "The time frame in which you confront issues determines, to a great extent, the outcome."

As leaders, we must not avoid confrontation, but we do need to learn how to evade it. There is a fine line between these two things. Avoiding confrontation is to close your eyes and act as if it is not there by never dealing with it. This only makes things worse. But evading confrontation is a strategic way to work your way around it, if possible.

I have found that most "problems" that occur dissipate after the emotional dust settles. Challenges cause an immense amount of dramatic debris. If not careful, leaders can turn molehills into mountains by reacting too quickly, in the moment, rather than responding collectively and calmly. Things can escalate rapidly if we try and deal with issues that, in fact, just need some time to resolve. Most people's confrontational emergencies are actually rooted from knee-jerk reactions to an issue. Leaders have to balance the art of knowing which battles to fight. Clearly not every time a bell rings does an angel get its wings, and not every time a bell rings does a boxing match have to start, either. Never avoid confrontation, but don't jump into it too quickly without assessing the severity of the situation. Timing is everything when it comes to confrontation.

2) Do Assume Responsibility

One of the greatest attitudes to display when confrontation occurs is that of responsibility. Genuinely looking in the mirror and realizing that your actions, or maybe even your inaction, may have caused the issue, is a sign of maturity and great leadership. Effective leaders live by the window and mirror principle. The window and mirror principle illustrates that when the team is doing great the leader looks out the window and gives the team all the credit. But when the team is doing poorly the leader willingly looks in the mirror and asks, "What do I need to do to be a better leader for my team?" Calling people out and quickly casting blame only causes others to back away from opening up. When you assume responsibility from the beginning, you are keeping people from becoming defensive. Some great statements to lead off with when you're dealing with confrontation is:

- Is there something I have done that has caused this to occur?
- It's very possible I have miscommunicated and caused some

confusion about this.

- I believe I might be missing the full context of what happened, could you clarify what took place so I can understand?
- What do you feel I need to know to fully understand this situation?

Notice how all of these statements assume responsibility with the word "I." It takes more strength to walk in humility than it does to stand in pride. The moment you start blaming people is the moment they will turn against you. Dr. Stephen Covey taught that to truly connect with people you have to first seek to understand in order to be understood.

3) Don't Let Yourself Get Drained

When dealing with challenges you can unknowingly get caught up in the negativity of the moment. You can easily start sinking in other people's quicksand. Leaders must stay above the fray. They have to keep their emotions and behaviors in check. Great leaders cannot let themselves become moody. If your attitude

> "Great leaders cannot let themselves become moody."

is unpredictable it creates confusion on the team and they won't know what to expect. Author Norman Vincent Peale said, "Nothing is more confusing than people who give good advice but set a bad example."

Leaders have to keep their cool even in adverse times. I remember a great scene in the movie *Six Days And Seven Nights* with Harrison Ford and Anne Heche. Picture the scene. The female character is a career-driven magazine editor on an island vacation, and the male character is a carefree pilot hired to take her home. As the plot rolls along, this duo ends up crashing on a deserted island. The woman goes into a state of panic as she tries to figure out how to survive, while the pilot keeps his laid-back attitude. At one point, the two of them climb to the top of the highest mountain on the island, hoping to find a beacon tower, only to find absolutely nothing.

In all calmness, Harrison Ford's character quietly goes into a nearby wooded area and starts yelling and shaking trees to unleash his frustrations. He then comes out relaxed and collected as Anne Heche's character looks at him with fear, thinking he has completely lost all control. She says, "Ever since we've been here you've been so confident. You have all the answers."

Harrison Ford responds, "Well, I'm the captain. That's my job. It's no good for me to go waving my arms in the air and screaming s***, we're gonna die!' That doesn't invoke much confidence, does it?"

I have always thought that scene was a great leadership illustration. The example you set is the example people will follow. Succumbing to every problematic situation consumes precious time and energy. Let your team know they need to deal with situations as they arise. The authority to resolve conflict should be pushed down to the lowest level possible in an organization. This means that people must be equipped and allowed to deal with confrontation throughout the entire authority chain. This will keep you from confrontational burnout. If nothing is getting dealt with, issues will keep rising to the top leaders and stall progress for the organization as a whole.

Your team needs the power and freedom to put out their own fires the way that you've agreed upon: The way that reflects the organization's values and vision. If every issue keeps coming back to you, the authority filter is too sparse. It is impossible for you, as the leader, to see all the conflict that goes on outside of your vantage point. This is why you must raise up self-sufficient leaders to deal with challenges at their level of responsibility. Putting out a fire inside one person is a whole lot easier than trying to put out a fire that has spread to a crowd. Challenge your team to solve their own problems so that every situation doesn't become your problem.

4) Do Use A Velvet Covered Brick

In the 1970s, author Howard Butt coined a phrase to help leaders understand how to deal with hard issues. He called it the "Velvet Covered Brick." The imagery was to help people understand that when dealing with conflict, there has to be a mixture of candor and care. We must not forget that we, as leaders, are here to connect with others for the greater good, not to criticize them. Too many leaders spend the majority of their time criticizing rather than connecting. This constant criticizing causes their influence to diminish. We can't allow frustrations to control our behavior. Never lash out from anger or bitterness. Let the dust settle enough to deal with the issue with a clear mind and a settled attitude. Many high quality employees have been emotionally decimated through the rage of explosive tempers that have come through uncontrolled leadership that is all brick and no velvet.

Our youngest daughter, who was five at the time, was doing a school assignment one day. She was reading about a character named Reddy the Fox, a mischievous animal being raised by his greedy grandmother. Grandma Fox was teaching Reddy how to capture the chickens at Bowser the Hound's farm. Allie's assignment was to write a letter to Reddy the Fox to try to help him become a better and more responsible fox. Here's what she wrote:

Dear Reddy Fox,

It's bad the way that you're doing stuff. You have to stop stealing those chickens. It's bad to try to kill the dog. Your Granny is evil. Your friends are smarter than you. You should never show Blacky the Crow tricks to make Bowser the Hound die.

Your friend,
Allie

I would say that's about as candid as it gets. She definitely cut to the chase, and then made sure she ended it with...your friend. Wouldn't it be nice if we could be so blunt, yet friendly and it be well received? It's never fun for a leader to deal with the rough, tough, and gruff challenges that people bring—but it is vital. Nobody wakes up each morning hoping to confront others and deal with conflict, but it happens, and somebody's got to do it. Jack Welch, CEO of General Electric said, "Be candid with everyone."

Whenever you are dealing with conflict remember this: You're doing the right thing by being candid when you do it with extreme care. When you truly care about the organization and the people in it you can always be guided by your genuine intentions. Even if people misunderstand you or simply don't agree with you, you will always know that you did what you thought was best for the situation and for the betterment of the person. Will you always get it right in how you deal with every situation? No, but you can rest at night knowing that you were carefully candid in your approach. Remember this rule: People trust those who are honest with them.

> "The heart of being candid is not about whipping your team; it is about equipping your team."

I have heard it said that a good leader is one who can step on your toes without messing up your shine. The better you deal with conflict the less room it has to grow out of control. The heart of being candid is not about whipping your team; it is about equipping your team. When you approach conflict with the agenda of helping rather than hurting then trust will arise over time. Poet Kahlil Gibran said, "Tenderness and kindness are not signs of weakness and despair, but manifestation of strength and resolution." Great leaders do not treat their people like robots and machines; they treat them more like family and friends.

Questions To Think About:

A) What is the difference between avoiding confrontation and evading it?

_____

_____

_____

B) Why should leaders start with assuming responsibility when dealing with confrontation?

_____

_____

_____

C) List two to three areas of confrontation you need to address next in your leadership?

1._____

_____

2._____

_____

3._____

_____

Leadology Challenge:

Chances are, there are conversations out there you have been putting off; issues that need to be addressed that you have hoped would just disappear. With the exception of a handful, most people tend to avoid confrontation. But if you want to move you and your team forward, it will require vulnerability and candidness.

Make a list of the things you need to address and start working through them one by one. You may want to snowball the issues, so start with the smallest ones and work your way up to the larger issues. Snowballing hard issues allows for you to build up courage as you knock out the little things quickly.

Always ask the question, "What would a great leader do in this situation?" This question can be a guiding light for you while navigating through hard times. It helps to remove your emotions and personal attachments to the issues. The question also helps to clarify what the right thing to do is.

THE CHESS GAME

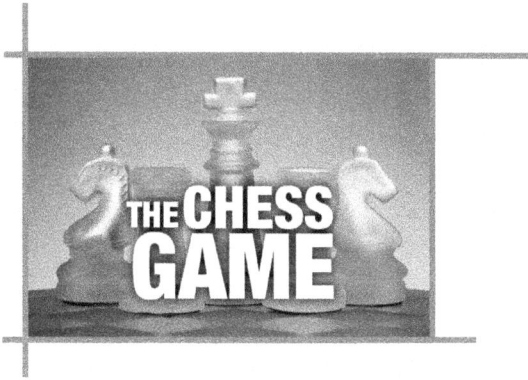

The Chess Game

Everyone operates from a distinct skill set that only they possess. Getting the right people in the right position can mean the difference between winning or losing. When leaders know their team members' strengths and unique abilities, they can maximize the overall success of their organization.

While growing up, I was very competitive with my father when it came to games. When I was old enough to learn, my dad taught me how to play chess. I was excited about the fact that I had matured from checkers to the big leagues. I wrongly assumed, however, that chess was just the adult version of checkers and that I could figure it out quickly. Little did I know how different the two games were.

In chess, every piece moved differently than the others, and it took me a while to get used to the complex system. My dad took the time to teach me the technique and strategy needed to win.

Over time I better understood the game, and I was finally able to keep up with Dad. Our games would get pretty competitive as I would always trash-talk him and try to taunt him with my self-declared fierce mind skills. Little by little I was gaining ground, and game-by-game I was getting closer to being able to put him in checkmate.

The day of my victory finally came. I will never forget it. It was glorious! Dad probably thinks he made a mistake somewhere, but really it was just me outwitting him all along. Actually, I am not sure if I earned the victory or he allowed me to win for my confidence. More than likely it was the latter. I like to think it was because of my amazing skills that overpowered him mentally that I took home the victory, but he might have a different perspective on that. However, I still claim he was no match for my mind power to this day!

I learned a very important lesson about leadership over those years of playing chess with Dad. You see, leading people is best understood when looking at the difference between checkers and chess. In checkers, every piece moves the exact same; however, in chess the pieces move according to their unique ability. Leaders that treat everyone the same, as in checkers, will put a lid on their own leadership effectiveness and a lid on the person they are leading. The leader that operates from a checkers perspective will not be able to get the most out of their team. But when a leader treats their team like chess pieces and seeks to know each person's unique wiring and skill set, they will be able to maximize the greatest strengths within the team. Leaders have to mature from leading in their own preferred way, to leading in the way those on their team need to be lead, just like I had to mature from checkers to chess. This is a vital concept to understand when it comes to being a great leader. What works to drive one person may be totally different from what works to drive another person.

I can't tell you how many times I've heard leaders say, "This is how I lead, people need to deal with it!" Although there is a truth that employees need to partially mold to the leader's style, the same applies to the leader. The leader has to partially adapt their style to what fits their people as well. Just like any relationship needs give and take to make it work, leaders and team members need to work together in their relationship to achieve a successful balance. This balance is all about getting the right people in the right place on the team. Great leaders develop the ability to identify the right person for the tasks at hand. They become master chess players who are able to move people to the right places.

Chessmaster Paul Morphy said, "Help your pieces so they can help you." If you don't have the right people in place it is impossible to get the best from them. It is painfully obvious when the wrong person is set in the wrong place. I came across these humorous employee performance reviews that illustrate the brutal truth when someone is not cutting it.

- Since my last report, he has reached rock bottom, and has started to dig.
- Works well, when under constant supervision and cornered like a rat in a trap.

151

- When he opens his mouth, it seems that this is only to change whichever foot was previously in there.
- He would be out of his depth in a parking lot puddle.
- She sets low personal standards, then consistently fails to achieve them.
- This employee should go far—and the sooner he starts, the better.
- Gates are down, lights are flashing, but the train just isn't coming.
- Wheel is turning, but the hamsters are all dead.
- Takes him an hour and a half to watch 60 Minutes.
- Got a full six-pack, but lacks the plastic thingy to hold it all together.
- A photographic memory, but with the lens cover glued on.
- Some drink from the fountain of knowledge; but he only gargles.
- If you give him a penny for his thoughts, you'd get change.

The greatest obstacle to progress is having the wrong people trying to move the organization forward. If you want your organization to advance, it is imperative that you have

> "If you want your organization to advance, it is imperative that you have the best people working to make it happen."

the best people working to make it happen. There is a specific method that I have come up with which helps leaders know how to get the right people in the right place. I call this "The Performance Formula." When someone is not operating in the proper formula there is chaos in the organization. Here is "The Performance Formula" to help you evaluate if you have the right people with the right skill in place:

Wrong Person + Wrong Skill – Disaster

Wrong Person + Right Skill = Frustration

Right Person + Wrong Skill = Burnout

Right Person + Right Skill = Fulfillment

Wrong Person + Wrong Skill = Disaster

Nothing is more disastrous to a team than an individual who operates with bad chemistry and the wrong skill set for the job. Everyone loses when this combo is active on the team. This type of person needs to find a fit somewhere else in the organization, or more than likely, in another organization. They do not fit the culture nor do they possess the abilities it takes for the tasks to be executed.

They will consistently be a hindrance to everyone and themselves. The longer people are allowed to operate from this formula, the more disastrous it is for the organization. Lead with speed and move this person quickly.

Wrong Person + Right Skill = Frustration

Even though an individual may have great talents and skills, it does not mean they have the right chemistry for the team. If a person is highly skilled but does not carry the DNA of the culture, tension will eventually build up between them and everyone else. The tension will come from the lack of relationship and morale that is vital for success. This type of person will get things done, but they will not have any connection outside of their responsibilities. They won't last long, unless they can begin to be part of the relational culture. Team members will feel defragmented from one another. Skill can never take the place of character and chemistry. Teamwork trumps talent over time.

Right Person + Wrong Skill = Burnout

When the right person with the right chemistry is operating outside of their strength zone, they will eventually burn out. They will begin to feel overwhelmed by the demands they are not able to meet. Even though they have great chemistry for the team, it does not automatically mean they are being utilized in their greatest abilities. At first, the team will be excited about this person based on the synergy, but over time the person's inability to get things done will weigh them down and cause the team to drag.

These people can most likely stay on the team, but they need to find their niche and stay within their strengths. Albert Einstein said, "Everybody is a genius. But if you judge a fish by its ability to climb a tree, it will live its whole life believing that it is stupid." Don't have the right person doing the wrong job. Make sure everyone is operating from their sweetest spot.

Right Person + Right Skill = Fulfillment

When the right person with the right gift fits with the culture of the team there is magic! They will feel fulfilled in what they are able to do because of high competency and high chemistry. Fulfillment is key to getting people set up for the long haul of making an impact in the organization. People in this category will perform at their highest level. They are a joy and they bring joy to those they work with.

This kind of person is necessary for an organization to grow to its fullest potential. These people add value to the overall success of everyone. They are high capacity players who know their strengths and stay in that zone. You don't have to ask if this is the right person and right skill; you already know. Coach Lou Holtz said, "I have coached good players and I have coached bad players. I'm a better coach with good players." Great organizations are great because they get everyone to operate from this formula.

There is no need to encourage someone to continue on when they are working in the wrong zone. This will only drive them to disaster, burnout, or frustration. However, when people are placed in their strength zone they will be in the sweet spot of success. It unifies the team when a leader finds the right mix of people. When you recognize others' strengths, you know where they will fit best. People who are operating in their strength zone will accomplish more in a shorter amount of time and have better results. If a leader fails to recognize others' strengths, that leader will create an unhealthy environment disconnecting people from their ability to perform.

Instead of people feeling connected to their work, they will start resenting it. Always focus on a person's strengths more than their weaknesses. Develop their strengths and delegate their weaknesses. Author, columnist, and playwright, Marilyn vos Savant said, "Success is achieved by developing our strengths, not by eliminating our weaknesses."

Here are a few questions to ask that will help you discover the strengths within an individual:

What Are They Passionate About?

The areas people are most passionate about usually involve their strengths. Simply listening to the ideas that ignite their excitement will give you clues to their unique gifts. Find out what they read about, think about, and ask questions about. These insights will help you know their true passions. When you find someone's passion, you will find what they will be most productive in. The goal is to

> "When you find someone's passion, you will find what they will be most productive in."

connect their passions with their job responsibilities. The larger the gap is between someone's passion and their work, the less productive they will be. Leonardo da Vinci said, "Where the spirit does not work with the hand there is no art." The less of a gap there is between someone's passion and their job, the easier it is to activate them. Bridging an individual's passion to their job self-motivates them to be internally invested in their work.

What Have They Succeeded At In The Past?

It doesn't matter what people have talked about doing; what matters is what they have successfully done. To find someone's strength, look to his or her achievements. What tasks, events, programs, or opportunities have they excelled in? Success in a particular area indicates an individual's strength. People do not excel in things they are bad at. This is especially important with new team members. Find out what they have done well in the

156

past and develop those things for the future. As they continue on, make sure you get the stats and keep the stats so that you, as the leader, are aware of individuals' best performances.

You can't manage what you don't measure.

As they finish tasks and projects you have assigned to them, make sure to take notes on how they did. Be specific about the areas they executed well and the areas they struggled with. Reflecting upon past performance gives you great insight into future possibilities. I would also encourage you to test individuals' abilities by letting them take on new roles. You never know what hidden strength or talent they may have buried within them just waiting to be unleashed.

What Comes Easily To Them?

We are naturally intuitive in the area of our strengths. When someone is able to learn a new skill quickly or accomplish assignments efficiently, it is usually a great indicator of their strengths. Find out what comes easily to others and make note of it. What do they accomplish faster than anyone else? What do they inherently know faster than others? This can be an "x factor" type of characteristic that people have in their strength zone. They just have that "gut feeling" that seems to guide them in their decision making.

Neuroendocrinologist Dr. Deepak Chopra says, "If you say 'I have a gut feeling about such and such' you're not speaking metaphorically, you're speaking literally. Your gut makes the same chemicals that your brain makes when it thinks." When someone says, "I have a gut feeling" they are actually referring to the sensation they get as experiences, ideas, and decisions are activating. People have strong gut feelings in their areas of expertise. Know what your team members naturally are gifted with and get them in those areas of expertise.

What Do They Make Better?

When someone has strength in a given skill, they are clearly good at it. If you want to know if they are gifted in an area, give them something to do and see if they make it bigger or smaller. Highly gifted individuals will take a project and add to it rather than subtract from it. They will tend to be more thorough in the execution than average. Though we all need training to grow better, natural strengths lie within each person making them better at certain things.

People talk about the excellence that comes from this person. Others notice their performance. So listen to teammates and those around that particular individual. This may help you identify what areas this person goes above and beyond in. When someone has strength in an area, they make that area better and bigger as a result. Walt Disney said, "Whatever you do, do it well. Do it so well that when people see you do it they will want to come back and see you do it again and they will want to bring others and show them how well you do what you do." Find the kind of people that do what they do very well and let them do it!

Do not waste time focusing on people's weaknesses. Rarely will someone grow beyond average in a weakness. With an extreme amount of training and time, they may go from a two to a four in their weakness, but they will not go near a ten. They are weak in that area for a reason; it's simply not how they are wired. But if you can take their strength from a seven to a nine, or an eight to a ten, they will become invaluable. Why spend your time developing average when you could be developing an expert in their strength zone? Focus on the strengths of your team and capitalize on those strengths. Don't try to force pawns into becoming bishops. And certainly don't try to turn bishops into pawns. Know what your people are good at and keep them in the right performance formula. As leadership expert Jim Collins taught, you have to get the right people, on the right bus, and in the right seat. If your organization's mission is to climb trees would you rather hire a squirrel or train a horse? As the leader, you have to set up your team as a chess game and position everyone correctly so everyone comes out a winner.

> "If your organization's mission is to climb trees would you rather hire a squirrel or train a horse?"

Questions To Think About:

A) How do you currently assess if the right people are operating with the right skill in their duties?

_____

_____

_____

B) How can you discover strengths within an individual?

_____

_____

_____

C) List 2-3 ways you can be a better leadership chess player by maneuvering your team strategically.

1._____

_____

2._____

_____

3._____

_____

Leadology Challenge:

The right team will catapult your success; the wrong team will cripple it. You need to take a hard look at your team and assess whether you have the right people, in the right places, doing the right things. Sit down with the people you lead and make sure they are in the right spot. Discover their strengths and weaknesses. You may only be utilizing 70% of what they are capable of. Discovering their passion and where they add the most value is what great leaders spend their time doing.

Also, keep in mind that people change over time. You need to always be reevaluating your team every few years at minimum. Spend some time assessing them based on The Performance Formula, and make sure you have the right people, with the right skills, operating at their best. You may find some changes that need to be made or might even uncover new opportunities your people can engage in. Being a master leadership chess player requires a genuine understanding of how your team operates as individuals, and collectively as a whole. Position them correctly and you'll win—you'll win big.

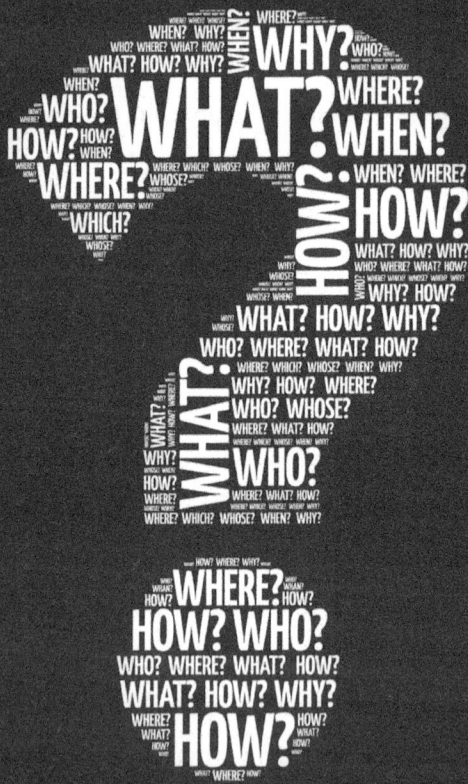

The
Qũéśţiōn
mark

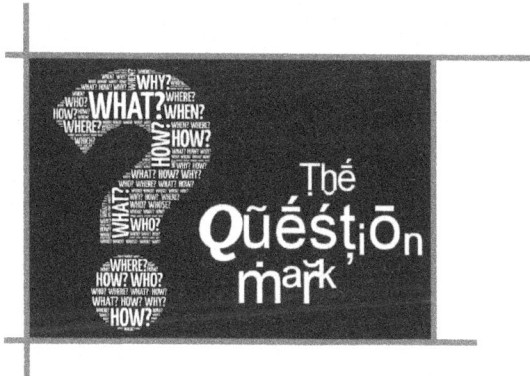

The Question Mark

The ability to ask extraordinary questions distinguishes great leaders from average leaders. An individual's impact will only go as far as the questions they are willing to ask. If you want to simply make an impression, answer questions; if you want to make an impact, ask them.

Years ago, I was invited to be a guest speaker at a large conference in Southern California. This was a great opportunity to add value to the attendees and share the stage with other great communicators. I looked forward to spending some time with the other speakers that were more seasoned and further along in their careers than me. I couldn't wait to rub shoulders with these leaders and learn from them. So, with great anticipation, I flew out to the venue and was transported to the hotel to check in for the weekend.

While I was checking in, I met one of the other guest speakers in the lobby. After introducing ourselves, we immediately jumped into a great conversation. I could tell he was a fantastic communicator as well as just an all around great guy to connect with. Our interaction really spurred an excitement in me to glean from this man's wisdom and experience. That night, he happened to be the keynote speaker to kick off the event, and I was amazed at his ability. His talk blew the roof off the building and, again, I was even more anxious to spend some one on one time with him.

After the event, we ran into each other back at the hotel and he asked if I would have breakfast with him the next morning before the event started back up. As I am sure you could guess by now, I was ecstatic about the opportunity. As I went to bed that night, I was mulling over all of the questions I wanted to ask him. I figured this was my shot to get in as much learning as I could. The next morning, I got ready, headed down to the restaurant, and spotted Mark waiting for me; ready to go. We sat down and chit-chatted a bit, and then right when I was getting ready to let this experienced and seasoned professional pour into a fresh young learner like me, he began asking me questions.

And not just questions, but questions he had prepared for me to help him. He asked me about my experiences; about the top leadership lessons I had ever learned, about books I'd been reading, and a host of other questions. I couldn't believe what was happening. Why was this man, much older and much more experienced than I am, asking me for tips and insights as though I had something to teach him? He sat there the whole time asking and listening. And not only did he listen, but as I answered his questions, he was genuinely writing things down that I had said. As I continued on, he kept encouraging me and building me up by showing gratefulness for the insight I was sharing with him.

When we finished breakfast and separated for the day, I just sat there stunned by what had happened. Why would this guy want to hear anything I had to say when he was clearly the one who had more answers than I did? Why was he so interested in listening and learning from a young pup like me? I felt amazing. I felt brilliant. I felt valued. I felt bigger on the inside. I felt inspired. I felt like I could take on the world. The questions also helped me untangle my thoughts and form ideas as I communicated. I actually learned more about myself as I answered his questions. And it made me think Mark was one of the most amazing men I had ever met.

Then it hit me...what made Mark so successful and influential was his ability to lead by asking questions. I had just met the man and I was willing to work for him, even as a volunteer if need be.

Socrates taught that the quality of the questions we ask will determine the quality of life we live. Asking questions will take you further in life than answering them. Show me someone who is good at asking questions and I will show you someone who will be successful. As leaders, we influence others by intentionally interacting with them. Questions create an engaging transaction of thought and response. The greatest leaders are the ones who lead with questions. In fact, great leaders spend more time asking questions than they do providing answers. As author Bob Tiede said, "Leadership is not as much about knowing the right answers, as it is about knowing the right questions."

Over the years, we have been led to believe that leaders are those who walk boldly, accumulate power, bark out orders, and make decisions for everyone to carry out. But that is simply not the case anymore. Today's leader is the one who asks great questions, listens very carefully, strategizes collaboratively, and builds consensus among all those necessary for achieving results. Woodrow Wilson said, "The ear of the leader must ring with the voices of the people."

Remember, God gave us two ears and one mouth for a reason; to listen twice as much as we talk.

> "The greatest leaders lead by listening to what others are communicating."

Listening creates a feedback loop that equips us to make proper assessments. Assuming you know without truly knowing can cause false assessments that produce flawed results. The greatest leaders lead by listening to what others are communicating. A leader does not try to do everything by themselves—they get things done by helping others lead themselves. Inspiring others to be driven drives them. Leaders are not the ones who do all the great work; they are the ones who help raise up others to do even greater work. They are multipliers, figuring out new ways to get more done through empowering those around them.

One of the most empowering strategies a leader can use to listen and raise up others is to ask questions. A great leader spends the majority of their time asking rather than telling. Just the other day, I was meeting with a friend of mine who is an engineer at one of the largest pharmaceutical companies in America. As we were having dinner, he shared with me how he leads his team by asking three very insightful questions:

1) What is one thing I can do for you to help you with your job?
2) How well do you think you are doing in your role, based on feedback you have received?
3) What are your strengths and weakness, based on feedback you have received?

By asking these questions, he is able to lead his team more effectively. Instead of assuming he knows what to do *for* them; he asks them what they need *from* him. Instead of *telling* them how they are doing in their job performance, he first *asks* them how they think they are doing. Instead of *creating* a list of their strengths and weaknesses, he prompts them to *discover* who they are. When you ask your team questions it allows them to engage. If someone escapes a conversation without thinking for themselves, they will never improve their ability to solve problems and extract solutions.

Questions educate and develop. In fact, the word *educate* comes from the Latin word *educo*, meaning to draw out from within. The only way to truly educate others is to help them think for themselves. If you do all the thinking, all of the work, and all of the problem solving, you are not developing those around you. To help draw out the potential from within an individual, it takes leaders who *educo* others, meaning they challenge the individual to think for themselves. We have all heard the famous phrase, "Give a man a fish you feed him for a day, but teach him how to fish and you feed him for a lifetime."

Only a true leader could coin this phrase, because at the heart of leadership is an ability to draw out the gold from the mines within another. Empowerment comes from educating. That is exactly what Mark did with me; he asked questions and it caused me to learn about myself. Not only did I learn about myself, but because he listened, and cared, it made me think all the more of him.

Benjamin Disraeli and William Gladstone were two of the most politically competitive rivals in nineteenth-century Great Britain. Battles between them were so intense in the political arena that it flowed over to their personal lives. They were both animated men who were experts in politics. Still, Benjamin Disraeli beat Gladstone and became the victor as Prime Minister in the end. What separated the two rivals, apart from their political beliefs, was Disraeli's ability to connect with others. The difference is best illustrated by the account of a young woman who dined with both men on consecutive nights. When asked about her impression of the rival William Gladstone, she said, "When I left the dining room after sitting next to Mr. Gladstone, I thought he was the cleverest man in England, but after sitting next to Mr. Disraeli, I thought I was the cleverest woman in England."

Dr. Stephen Covey said, "When you really listen to another person from their point of view, and reflect back to them that understanding, it's like giving them emotional oxygen." A leader that never listens is a leader that will never be listened to.

> "A leader that never listens is a leader that will never be listened to."

Let me give you two diagrams that illustrate the power of questions. The first one is the traditional and most common way people lead (leading with answers). The second flips the model and shows how highly successful people lead (leading with questions).

Model #1 – Leading With Answers

Let's use this diagram (1A) as a typical meeting in which the leader and the team are discussing whatever it is they are discussing. Usually the leader is the one conducting the meeting as everyone is looking to, and relying upon them for answers and direction.

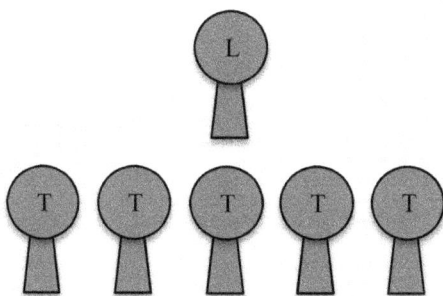

1A

Answers Go Down

Typically, the leader begins by telling everyone (diagram 1B) what he or she wants done, why he or she wants it done, and how he or she wants it done. The leader is giving answers to anticipated questions from everyone on the team. In this model, the leader is doing a lot of talking and probably expecting the team to be taking notes on all the information that he or she is rattling off.

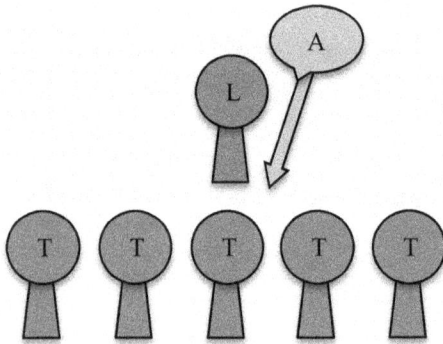

1B

Questions Come Up

Now that the leader has spoken and given everyone their marching orders, the leader then says something to the effect of, "Any questions?" The team is expected to clear up anything fuzzy by getting their one moment of clarification in before the rat race starts. Sometimes the leader says, "This is it, now is the time to ask any questions, or else it's go time." If the team is bold, they will risk the embarrassment of looking lost, confused, and incompetent by raising their hand to ask vulnerable questions. Or perhaps they will simply say "no" when, in fact, they have tons of questions. Many leaders actually think they did a great job in the meeting if no one had any questions. They pat themselves on the back believing they did a superb job at anticipating the questions people may have had by preemptively answering them.

Basically, in this traditional model of leadership (as seen in diagram 1C), answers go down from the leader and questions come up from the team. This is how most people have been taught, and it is the experience many have in their current work environment; but there is little engagement, and virtually no room for dialogue and disagreement. The model that highly effective leaders use is the total opposite. Let's look at how great leaders flip the model:

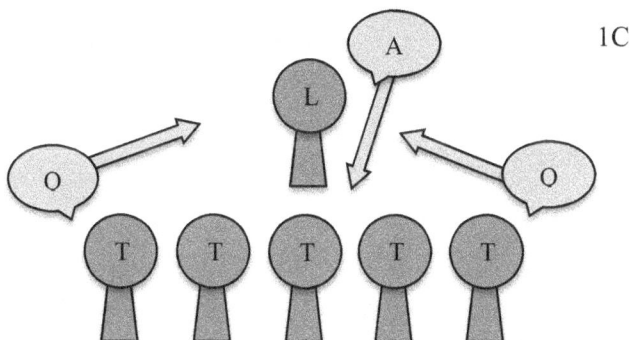

1C

Model #2 – Leading With Questions

As the diagram shows in 2A, everyone is looking to and relying upon the leader as in model #1. This still holds true. Leaders need to be visible and accessible to their people as they provide direction.

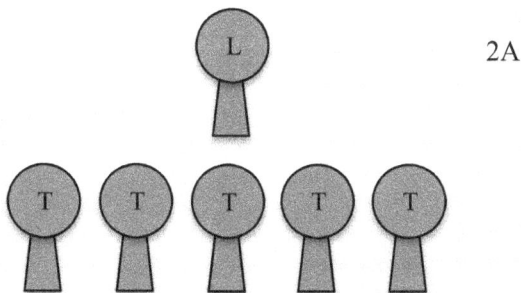

2A

Questions Go Down

It all flips in this step. Instead of answers going down and questions coming up, questions go down and answers come up as in diagram 2B. Great leaders ask great questions, so the leader begins by asking their team about important details, data, and possible decisions that have been or need to be made. The leader begins to engage people by digging into their areas of responsibility. The leader avoids asking closed-ended questions. This means staying away from questions that can only be answered with yes or no responses. They instead ask questions that spur dialogue such as:

- Where are you at with project x?
- What do you feel is an appropriate deadline to get task x finished?
- What are the top 2-3 obstacles that are holding you back from accomplishing idea x?
- What specific steps do you need to take to get to x?

These types of questions allow the team to engage in conversation. Asking questions that result in yes or no answers never allows the leader to find out more that may be going on behind the curtain.

2B

Answers Come Up

Now that the leader has pitched their questions toward the team, the team is expected to start batting answers back to the leader. The team must engage and elicit answers from what has been asked of them. This is when the magic really happens; the team has an opportunity to open up and participate in the process of creating. When someone is part of the creating process they are much more likely to take ownership in the outcome. They feel a part of the development and solution for the issues at hand. Leading is about developing your people to think and do. So the leader should be asking the questions and the team should be offering up the answers as in diagram 2C.

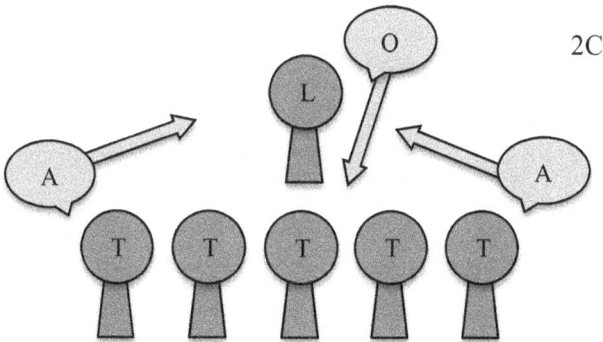

2C

By asking questions, the leader is accomplishing multiple results:

- They are gaining clarity and intel about what is going on in each team member's respective area(s).
- They are making it clear that team members need to be prepared to bring something to the table.
- They are bringing accountability to everyone by providing an opportunity for team members to communicate about their areas. This lets the entire team hear what is going on, which creates a healthy social vulnerability.
- They are coaching their team by allowing them to process their own thoughts, tasks, goals, and deadlines.
- They are allowing their team to do the work, thus freeing the

173

leader up to commit to other tasks.

To develop your team, you must develop their ability to interact with problems and solutions. The more questions you ask, the greater your team will become. The most limiting behavior a leader can operate from is that of a "know-it-all" who appears to have an answer for everything. "Know-it-alls" need no team; they simply want slaves. Slavery is not teamwork; teamwork requires contribution. The greater the dream, the greater the team needs to be. And the greater the team, the more answers they will bring to the table. If your team is not bringing solutions, then you are either leading them ineffectively or they are not the right team.

> "Slavery is not teamwork; teamwork requires contribution."

Knowing how to ask a question is vital to your leadership ability. Let me give you a great acronym to use when you A.S.K. questions:

A = Articulate The Question

Be very clear and precise about the questions you ask. The quality of your questions will determine the quality of the answers you receive. Unclear questions get unclear answers. Be strategic and intentional about how you craft your questions. The vaguer your questions are, the harder it is for people to respond to them. Instead of saying, "How's project x going?" which is a very vague and subjective question, ask something more specific, like, "What are the top two components that are causing project x to move forward?" Follow that up with, "What are the top two obstacles that might be causing it to move slower than it should?" These are much more specific and engaging questions that elicit authentic and objective responses. They also help prioritize the most important factors at play. The way a question is asked is as important as the answer you seek to receive. Remember: the goal is to engage the person with questions that draw out answers. Open-ended questions draw out answers. Lawyers are trained to ask open-ended question to friendly witnesses for that reason, and closed-ended questions to hostile witnesses.

S = Seek Out Appropriate Contributors

Asking the right question to the wrong person will give you the wrong data. Make sure that you are asking the appropriate people the appropriate questions. I witness many leaders who become misinformed because they counsel with the wrong people. Who you direct your questions to is just as important as the question itself. Getting to the right contributors will begin to direct you to the right information. Asking the wrong person the right question can be frustrating, both to you and to the person you asked. If you truly want to learn, seek out those who have the right perspective on the matter. And always seek out multiple sources.

Many senior leaders are blind to the truth, because they only ask questions of the person who directly reports to them. That direct report can easily be skewed based on the person's perspective, attitude, and fears they may have concerning the issue. Only asking the overseer of a project how things are going can give you a one-sided answer. Make sure you get 360-degree answers by engaging various people, not just one person. A great leader asks several people the right questions to gain a holistic view of how things are going. Be very selective about directing the right questions to the right persons. Knowing who you are talking to and what you want to draw out from within them should guide the questions you engage them with.

K = Know What To Do With The Answers

Getting answers to your questions doesn't mean much if you're not going to do something about it. Sometimes you have to open up to other people's answers even if you disagree; especially if the majority of your inner circle is agreeing on something that you are not. A leader can ask great questions, but then tune out the answers if they are not careful. This does not mean you, as the leader, must act on every suggestion you receive. But it does mean you need to explore possibilities beyond your current level of awareness. Don't be too quick to shut down ideas and solutions just because you don't understand them at the moment.

If you consistently never use people's thoughts, ideas, and solutions, your team will begin shutting down. They will sense that you are only going to do what you want to do anyway, and that their input won't be valued. Martin Luther King Jr. said, "A genuine leader is not a searcher for consensus but a molder of consensus."

It's your job as a leader to take all the answers from your questions and mold them into a solution that is best. Sometimes, this requires you to trust others and do things outside your opinion, and sometimes outside of your comfort level. Author and civil rights advocate Lillian Smith said, "When you stop learning, stop listening, stop looking and asking questions, always new questions, then it is time to die."

As leaders, we must be open to listen to our team and act on the suggestions they provide.

Always lead with questions.

Questions To Think About:

A) How is leading with questions different from what you have been conditioned to lead with?

_____

_____

_____

B) Why is leading with questions such a powerful strategy?

_____

_____

_____

C) List three thoughtful questions you can use in the future.

1._____

_____

2._____

_____

3._____

_____

Leadology Challenge:

Questions are one of a leader's greatest assets. The more thoughtful questions you have in your quiver, the more bullseyes you can hit. But they keyword is: *thoughtful*. Questions are not all created equal. The old adage that says, "There's never a bad question," is not always true when it comes to leadership. You certainly don't want to belittle people or come across condescending as you question them. The art of asking great questions is about being intentional with the nature of the question.

There are too many kick-starter questions out there to list, so, I suggest you spend some time searching great questions leaders ask. Write down the ones that resonate with you. Write down the nature of what you are trying to extract. Have a running list of great questions that prompt you in conversations with your team. You can always look over these questions before a meeting and even have them listed somewhere for quick access. The important thing to remember is: know what questions you want to ask. Don't go into conversations without being prepared with thoughtful inquiries.

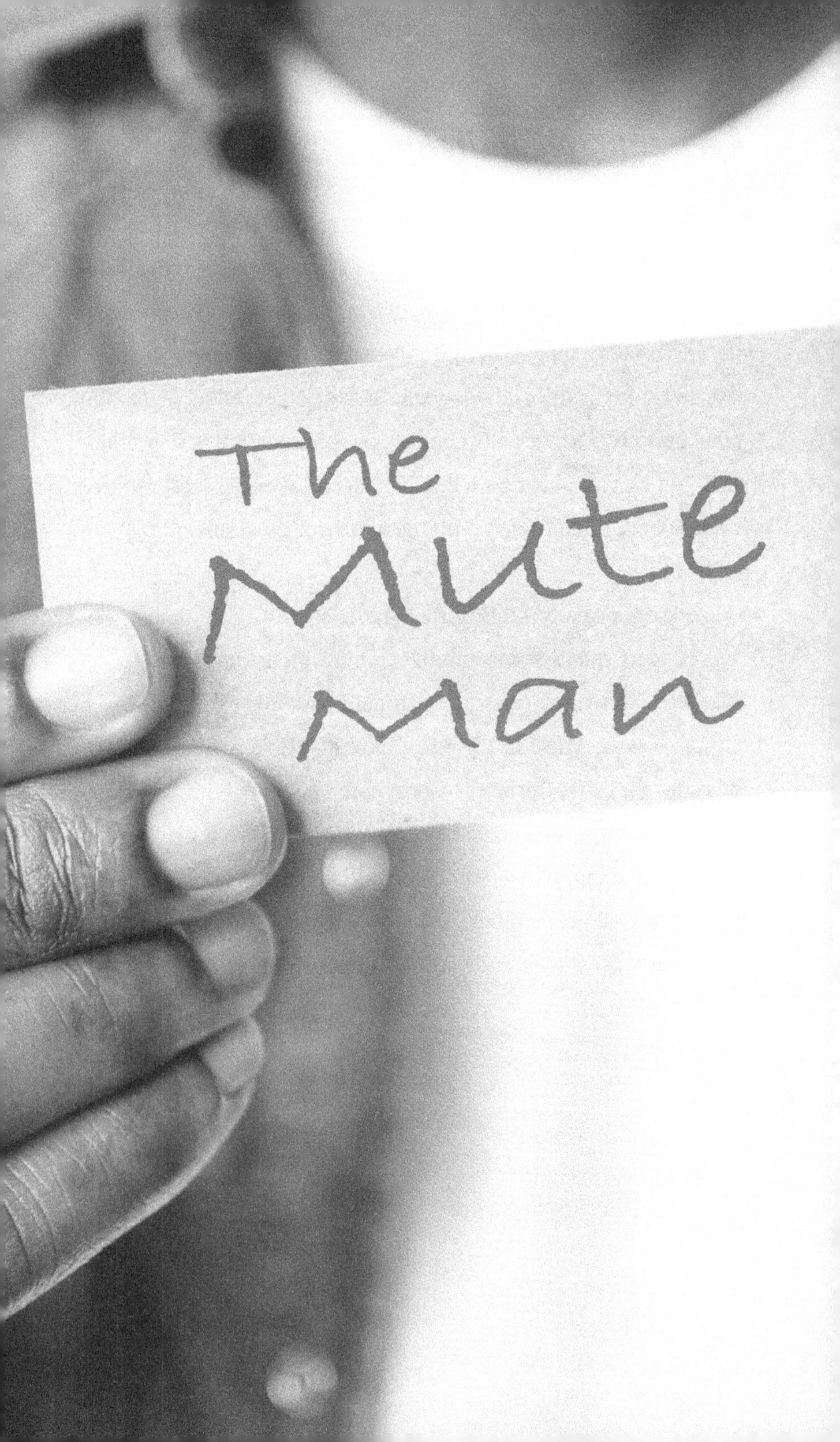
The
Mute
Man

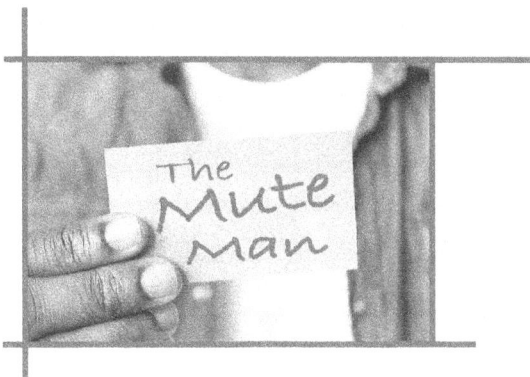

The Mute Man

How you communicate dictates the future you'll experience. What you say and how you say it will determine what you get and how you'll get it. Words have power—creative power, and destructive power. Great leaders understand and leverage the power of the tongue.

On the way home from work one day, I pulled into a Kmart to shop. Though I had in mind the few things I wanted to purchase, I somehow got sucked into browsing through the vast array of items I didn't need. As I was browsing around the store, taking my time, checking out all of the goods, I started noticing that the same middle-aged man kept appearing in nearly every aisle that I was in. I didn't think much of it...at first. I figured he was just another guy having a good time shopping Kmart's amazing deals.

Well, after about twenty minutes of me bumping into this guy everywhere, I turned and noticed that he wasn't browsing; he was actually following me from aisle to aisle and staring…at me. His head was tilted down and his eyes were locked onto me with laser beam focus. I began to feel my nerves tense up, but I kept my cool. Still, not completely sure that my mind wasn't playing tricks on me; I decided to really investigate my suspicion that this man was following me.

Were our meetings simply happenstance or did I have need for concern?

I began to walk through aisles quickly and stay on the move. There was no way this guy would be able to keep up with me unless he meant to. This was when things got creepy. As I sped up, so did he. The faster I went, the faster he went. At one point, his gaze met mine; his head was tilted even lower than it had been before and his eyes began glowing…well…at least, that's what was running through my mind as fact and fear started to intermingle.

I now reached the point of getting a little freaked out. I picked up my pace, just to make doubly sure this wasn't all in my head, but to my distress it clearly wasn't. Nope, this man was following me with intention and agenda. What his intentions and agenda were, I knew not, so my fast walking pace turned into a slow jog, and so did his. Are you kidding me? My jog turned into a quick dash down an aisle to accomplish my exit plan, but when I turned the corner to head down the next aisle, BAM, there was the man, at the other end of the aisle, staring me down like a gunslinger in a western showdown.

How did he get down there? Did he eat his Wheaties for breakfast? Is he going to try to attack me? Can I take him down? All of these thoughts came rushing into my mind in an instant. Then he started making a brisk walk toward me. We locked eyes. Everything went into slow motion. I think I even heard the theme song to *The Good, The Bad, And The Ugly* begin to play, but with a heavier twang than normal. Then he slowly began to reach into his inside shirt pocket. Was he going to pull a gun? A knife? Brass knuckles? As I braced myself to either dodge a bullet, counter block a knife thrust, or go hand-to-hand in combat with this stranger, he carefully pulled out a very small object.

At first, I wondered if it was a tricky, thin, Chinese star weapon of some sort. But as I got a better look, the item didn't look as dangerous as my imagination led me to expect. He stopped about two feet in front of me with his hand extended all the way to my chest, just staring at me with his tilted head. He was holding a business card out for me to take. I slowly looked at the card, then at the man, and then at the card again. He nodded as if to prompt me to take it from his hand. The situation seemed safe enough at this point, so I took the card. It read, "Hello."
That's it. I wasn't sure what to do, so I said, "Hello?"

He reached into his pocket and pulled out another card that read, "I am mute. I am raising money for our organization. Would you like to donate?"

All now became clear. This man was not trying to kill me, he was trying to petition for my charity. He was unable to speak and was simply raising money for his cause. I was relieved. I had never been so happy to have been asked for a donation in my life, though I could have thought of a hundred better ways to approach someone for a donation than make them fear for their life. Unfortunately, I only had some pocket change on me at the time. Still, I handed him all I had.

He seemed a bit frustrated—as if I was holding out. But I don't think he knew that I was probably in need of some donations myself. He must have expected much more since he singled me out and chased me around the store. In the end, he was grateful for my donation and even handed me another card that read, "Thank you!"

This interaction with the mute man taught me a valuable lesson about communicating. One of the most powerful tools we have is our capacity to communicate. The man had the right words on the cards, but delivered them in a distorted way. The way we communicate has the power to either:

Construct or Destruct
Build or Bulldoze
Empower or Implode
Motivate or Mutilate
Exonerate or Assassinate

Excellent communications makes the difference between average leaders and great leaders. When communication goes down, confusion comes up. If I could spend one day with you and your team, I would be able to tell how successful you will be based on what is communicated. You see, every organization has a language; a dialect in which they communicate. The narrative that is used will determine the result in which it produces.

> "When communication goes down, confusion comes up."

Words always produce results: good, bad, or indifferent. Words are constantly at work effecting outcomes. Once something is communicated, it is out there. The wave of impact that word has will continue to carry momentum long after it is heard. This is why we play back words and conversations in our heads long after the conversation has been finished. Author Napoleon Hill said, "Think twice before you speak, because your words and influence will plant the seed of either success or failure in the mind of another." Words are truly like seeds that will eventually produce sweet fruits or bitter roots. As leaders, we must be very careful and very intentional about the words we communicate.

Proverbs 18:21 says, "The tongue has the power of death and life." The more respect a person has, the more powerful their words become. What you say, and how you say it, determines what happens, and how it will happen. You will never see a highly successful leader or organization that communicates from a negative narrative. In fact, the reason they became successful is largely due to communicating life-giving words. However, you will always see struggling leaders and organizations consistently speaking from a negative, life-draining narrative. You will hear things like:

- We don't have what it takes to grow anymore.
- There isn't enough time in the day to get things done.
- I cannot take on one more thing.
- Aren't we doing enough already?
- People drive me crazy!
- I am so sick of how we do things!
- I can't wait till the weekend.
- It's good enough.
- People don't care…it's not that big of a deal, anyway.
- I'm so tired of dealing with problems around here.
- I am not going to do that; it's not in my job description.
- I wish people would pick up their slack around here. I'm tired of carrying their weight.
- If I have to deal with one more customer today, I am going to walk-out.

This type of language absolutely sabotages an organization. It eats success away like a cancer from the inside out. Negative narratives always produce toxic environments. Gossip, slander, backbiting, and negativity absolutely destroy people and organizations faster than any other force. If you're familiar with financial expert Dave Ramsey and his organization, you'll know that they have a strict no-gossip policy. If someone is found gossiping, they get one warning; after that, they're fired immediately. Here is how Dave's company describes it on their website:

Gossip is defined as discussing anything negative with someone who can't help solve the problem. If you're having computer problems, and IT is slow about helping you, you don't complain about it to the sales rep in the break room. You talk to your leader because he or she can and will do something about it.

There cannot be any tolerance for destructive words. The truth is, you attract what you talk about. If you talk negatively, you will draw more negativity. Misery loves company. And not just loves either; it's magnetized to it. But success also loves company, and is magnetized to it as well. What goes around comes around. Or in the context of communication…what goes out, comes back. Words are like boomerangs: whatever you throw will return even faster.

The word *communicate* actually comes from the Greek word *koy-no-neh'-o*. It means "to have fellowship with, or to be in harmony with." This is where we get the word *community*. The word *communicate* also has the Latin word *uni*, meaning, to be one with. Whatever we communicate is what we come into community with, or become one with. Communicating literally attracts its likeness. The way one talks will determine the way one lives.

Your words become the reality within you and around you. This is why great organizations such as Dave Ramsey's company and a host of other highly successful companies are very intentional about the power of their words. You'll hear phrases like:

- We are going to move forward.
- I'll figure out how to get more time or free up time.
- I'll figure out how to make it happen.
- Let's not settle for where we're at.
- People are our greatest asset.
- We have great strengths and we have some things we are going to improve.
- I love what I do.
- It will work… but can we make it better?
- Let's offer the best of what I've got and what we've got.
- Let's work together and figure out how to compliment each other.
- I appreciate our customer base; they are why we exist.

Great leaders at great companies use great words to build a great movement. The way we talk and who we talk to can make or break future opportunities. We need to learn how to speak in surround sound. By surround sound, I mean the ability to communicate with everyone all around us. Just like Dolby Digital created the 5-point surround sound system, we too need effective communication with 5 points of contact that surround us.

Let's break these down:

1) Yourself

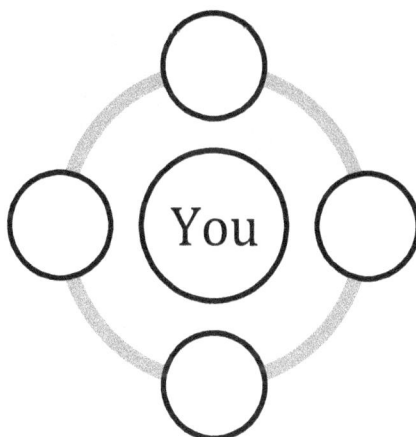

The most important person you'll ever communicate with is yourself. What you say to yourself will determine the confidence you exude. The way you talk directs your path. How you speak will determine how you lead. You can't speak failure over your life and expect to live successfully. If you constantly tell yourself that you are going to fail, chances are, you will. Keep making discouraging remarks about yourself and sure enough, you will own them.

> "You can't speak failure over your life and expect to live successfully."

This isn't just positive mumbo-jumbo hype; this is how we are created. The brain is made up of billions of pathways where information travels through at all moments. These pathways are constantly under construction in a term referred to as Neuroplasticity. Basically, your brain is ever-adapting and reinventing itself based on the information it is receiving. As new pathways are used, old ones begin breaking down.

This can be good news or terrible news, depending on what information your brain is currently processing. Environment, experiences, emotions, thoughts, and words have a tremendous impact on our ability to optimally function. What you consistently put into your brain is what begins to form in habitual pathways of activity. This is why we can learn new skills as we continuously practice them. Our old pathway of confusion and chaos begin to break down as we chart a new course of developing the skill. The nature of what you think about and what you say to yourself will literally rewire your brain.

Thus, your thoughts and words will become your new actions and habits over time. What you are communicating to yourself will wire your brain to produce an easy pathway to that result. If you constantly say and believe you aren't a creative person, you will actually create that behavior. Your brain will have a hard time being creative because it will flow to the unimaginative pathway you have constructed. If you consistently say you don't have enough resources to get something done, your brain will have a very difficult time trying to find the resources to get something done.

This is why we hit mental roadblocks when we are doing something we've never done; our brain is trying very hard to construct new pathways. If we give up and surrender to the pressure of negativity, we will stop constructing resourceful pathways and start constructing impossibility pathways.

You must reject the statement that you are somehow limited. The only limit you have is the belief that you have one. If you are destructive in the way you talk about yourself, you will be conditioned to live in a cage of uncertainty. Nothing good comes from negativity. Why waste our precious time talking about the negatives when we could talk about the positives? When you speak life and affirm your beliefs, you have laid the groundwork for success. Speak like the person you desire to become, not the person you currently are. What you talk about is what you will get.

> "The only limit you have is the belief that you have one."

Your self-talk shapes your self-worth. We all deal with the gremlin inside of us that is negative, grouchy, and fearful. Do not get comfortable with this pessimistic gremlin or it will take control of you. Build yourself up by speaking encouraging, positive, life-giving words over your future. You already talk to yourself, so make it a productive conversation.

2) Your Team

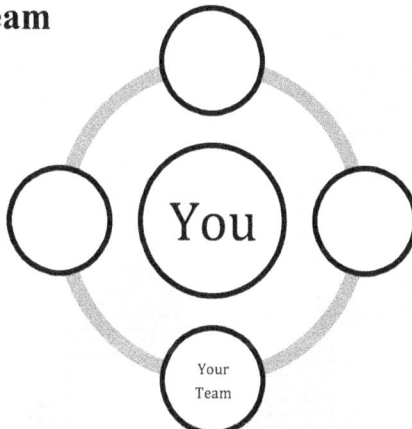

The way you communicate with your team determines how well they'll perform for you. Never talk down to your team; talk up to them. What I mean by "talking up" is building them up with your words. Treat them based on their potential. Speak to them with high expectations. Always be stretching them to the greatness they have within, just begging to be released.

My wife, Erin, and I have two beautiful daughters. When our youngest daughter was little, she would sometimes get an attitude when asked to do certain chores. Instead of obeying, she would work herself up to the point of getting upset. We would then have to discipline her and let her know that her behavior was unacceptable, but we didn't stop there. We wanted her to know that having a bad attitude was not true to who she really was. You see, our daughter was (and still is) a sweet and loving girl who truly wants to do good, but she was letting her emotions get the best of her. So, we would remind her that the attitude she was displaying was not like her.

We began to give her positive reinforcement by telling her how sweet she really was and that her current attitude did not reflect that. What were we doing? We were giving her an expectation to live up to. We could have simply said, "Why are you so angry when you have to do something? All you do is get upset when we ask you to do chores! Stop being an angry kid!"

But that would not have given her a good reputation to live up to. It would have given her the wrong expectation. She would have grown up thinking she was an angry person, and that could have turned into a perception of herself that she accepted. We made sure we spoke about her positive traits and not her negative ones. The great thing is that as she has grown older, she's started living up to the expectation we kept reinforcing in her. This positive expectation was so engrained in her over the years that now, when she has a slip up and starts to get upset, we can just look at her and she will say, "I know, that's not who I am."

If you want to give someone hope, give them an expectation they can aspire to reach. German writer, Johann Wolfgang von Goethe, said, "Treat a man

> "The best leaders are the ones who give people a great reputation to live up to."

as he is, he will remain so. Treat a man the way he can be and ought to be, and he will become as he can be and should be." When you communicate your belief in someone's potential, they will do their best to meet that expectation. The best leaders are the ones who give people a great reputation to live up to. Call people up to a higher level and the ones that can make it...will.

3) Your Peers

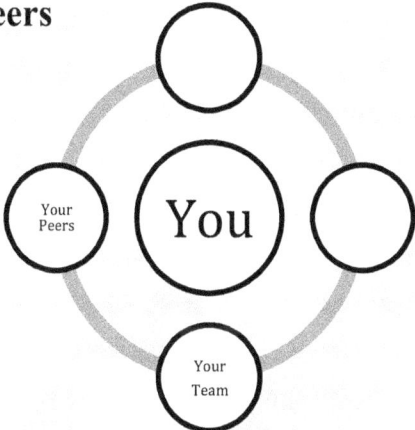

The way you talk to others and about them will determine the quality of relationship you have with them. Communicating from a place of togetherness creates teamwork. You have to put completing ahead of competing. The moment you start to compete with your peers is the moment you'll start to lose all influence with them. People need to feel that you are for them, not against them. Communicating the value of what they do, communicates the value of who they are. The more value you place on them, the more value they'll place on you. Always let the best idea win and give them credit for it. Make sure you publicly praise your peers among each other. Those who have the greatest influence are the ones who genuinely lift people up in front of others.

Be slow to accept all the praise, but quick to give it all away.

I had the chance to sit in on a company wide meeting for a very prominent organization not long ago, and what I witnessed was breathtaking. To start the meeting off, the senior leader opened up with what he called, "winning moments." This, apparently, was the way they kicked off every meeting. One by one, people stood up, pointed out someone else in the room, and then went on to give them a shout-out for how their performance the week before made a huge difference in the organization.

One guy said, "I just want to thank Jim for jumping in last minute to help us set up for a meeting we were running behind on. Jim, I know you were busy, but your effort made the meeting successful. Thank you for all your help!" Everyone then clapped and thanked Jim for his effort. This went on and on for about 20 minutes with everyone sharing big and little things people did that contributed to a great work environment. This organization was glowing with so much energy and excitement that I thought about putting in my resume.

After the "winning moments" time, the senior leader went on to talk about new initiatives that were coming down the pipe. His team welcomed what he shared with open arms and great anticipation. They truly used words to create a phenomenal environment that you couldn't help but be energized by. That senior leader could have easily dismissed the "winning moments" time and jumped right into his agenda, but he would have missed the chance to increase the peer-to-peer engagement of his team.

4) Your Superiors

When speaking to your superiors, use a supportive narrative. Let them know you're behind them and believe in them. Your words should communicate confidence in their leadership. If you begin to demean their leadership and decision-making, you'll start to work against them. If you can't get behind your leaders, you need to either step up and pull yourself together or step down and pull yourself out. It is impossible to value someone if you secretly feel they are a nobody. One of the most disastrous forces in an organization is loss of respect for superiors. The longer you stay in a place of frustration, the more toxic you will get. It is not fair for you or your superiors to continue on when it is time to go. How you talk about the people over you displays how you truly feel about them. It's one thing to not agree with decisions; it's a whole other thing to speak out against them. Though we all need to be up front and open with our ability to be vulnerable, we have to make sure we speak from a place of constructive criticism and not crippling condemnation.

Having the freedom to speak up is not about having the freedom to tear down.

If you want to have influence with your superiors and gain their ear, then use your words wisely. The more supportive of them you are, the more opportunity you will create. Great leaders are great followers. If you can't support your superiors, you'll have a hard time leading others. Never trust a person who isn't willing to support

> "If a person can't be led, they aren't fit to lead."

others. If a person can't be led, they aren't fit to lead. Opportunity doesn't knock on closed doors. Being disinterested in the vision and decisions of your leader will shut down your ability to grow.

Leaders need those who will lift their hands in battle. They need those who will go the extra mile to finish the race. They need those who will support their decisions and help advance the cause. Separating yourself from your superiors will only separate you from influencing them. However, when you gain the respect and trust of your superiors you will gain favor and influence with them. The more you communicate your confidence in your leaders the more confident they will be in you. Great leaders only hand responsibility down to those who they feel are able to carry it. There is a direct correlation between those who speak highly of their superiors and those who rise up in their organization.

5) Your Customers

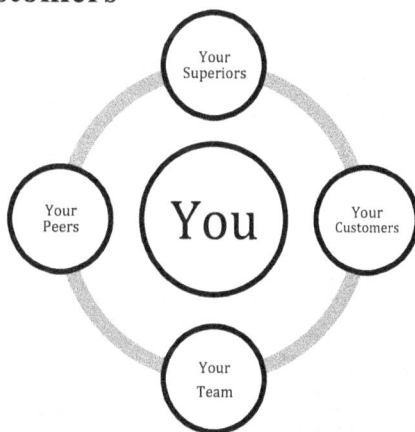

The people you service will either be drawn to you or be detracted from you based on how you communicate with them. In fact, studies have shown us that the tone in which people feel they are being communicated to with will determine their response. It's not just what we hear, but how we hear it said that impacts us. The University of Southern California conducted a two-year study on the effects of tone in communication. They put married couples through therapy sessions monitoring the pitch and intensity of their voices. The computer algorithm analyzed the data and, surprisingly, was a more accurate indicator of marital success than counseling professionals. After a five-year follow up with the participants, the computer algorithm was able to accurately confirm eventual improvements or declines in relationships 74% of the time.

How we use our words determines a great deal of the results we get. When talking with clients, customers, and prospects, our words can mean the difference between connecting and disconnecting. The "vibe" people feel is more reliable than we may give it credit. If people sense you are being genuine, they are much more likely to trust you. Change the way you talk, and you can change the opportunities you open up.

The other day, I was in our local Starbucks getting ready to order my favorite drink. As I walked up to the counter to let them know what I wanted, the lady taking my order spoke up and said, "A tall, non-fat, Caramel Machiatto, right?"

I enthusiastically responded, "Yes! How did you know?" I hadn't recognized this particular barista at my other frequent visits, but she was obviously new and already knew my order.

She told me that she remembered my drink and me from the week before when she was training with another barista. I was very impressed with her skills and it made me feel like an important customer. She went on to tell me that part of her training at this Starbucks was to always remember as many people's names and favorite drinks in order to make the customer's experience better. Well, I know that she succeeded, because I felt valued by her gesture. Her upbeat tone and genuine engagement made me respond with glee, meaning, I happily paid a lot of money for that tall latte.

Well played Starbucks, well played.

The truth is, our words and how we say them can either secure our ability to influence and secure business, or it can repel people away from our influence and business.

Leaders can't afford to communicate in a way that confuses, assumes, or maybe even scares others like the way the mute man did with me. The better you communicate the greater your ability to lead effectively.

Questions To Think About:

A) Rate which area of surround sound communicating you struggle with the most. Mark 1 for the hardest and 5 being the easiest...

Yourself____   **Your Team**____   **Your Peers**____

Your Superiors____   **Your Customers**____

B) Why do words have so much power?

_____

_____

_____

C) What are some buzzwords or phrases you want your organization to always be speaking?

_____

_____

_____

(Now that you have some buzzwords and phrases, implement them into the culture of your organization and make them known.)

Leadology Challenge:

Take inventory of the narrative of your words. Do you tend to speak positively or negatively in the surround-sound areas? Most people do well in a few and struggle in a few. The areas where you tend to be more verbally toxic are the areas you must look out for. Being inconsistent with your words disturbs the balance of your influence. Being negative in one area but positive in another does not balance you out. In fact, it actually dilutes your positivity and weakens your ability to communicate effectively. Speaking consistently positive in surround-sound skyrockets your influence and opportunities. In the case of words, it's a holistic endeavor, not a compartmentalized engagement. Your words have the power to live forever; thus, they must be handled with extreme care.

Start to level up your communication by taking control of your words. Catch yourself before speaking something that could be stated much better. Be cognizant of how you are talking and make a commitment to communicate the way that is in harmony with success.

The Symphony Orchestra

The
Symphony
Orchestra

The Symphony Orchestra

Leaders know that to orchestrate success they must come into harmony with what they seek to accomplish. Leadership is the metronome that keeps everything and everyone together; playing the same tune. When the right players are playing the right pieces, with the right point person, and at the right pace, a masterpiece of success resounds.

In my early twenties, I was invited by some friends to a university symphony orchestra concert. This was my first time attending such a "mature" event. I wasn't sure what to expect. After all, this wasn't the 90s grunge rock music I was accustomed to, but I agreed to go anyway, hoping some iconic rocker might be in attendance to make me feel more at home.

The night of the concert came and I got all dressed up like an adult. Instead of my usual baggy jeans and untucked shirt, I stepped up the game and decided to tuck in my shirt. This was my big step from rocker to refined gentleman. I was amazed that the place was packed when my friends and I arrived at the university auditorium.

Obviously, I was not aware of how many other young people in the world enjoyed this type of music. We made our way through the sea of people to the main doors, were handed our programs, and took our seats. Eventually, the concert began. Very quietly and somberly, an army of musicians, special guests, and an awkwardly excited conductor were introduced. Not sure of what kind of experience this was going to be, I braced myself for having to make the most of it.

Little did I know that this evening would turn out to be a turning point experience in my life; far beyond stepping out of my comfort zone to tuck in my shirttails. As soon as the first note thundered I was captivated. The sound, the power, the emotion, the variety of musicians and instruments; breathtaking! I watched in awe as the orchestra performed under the extremely enthusiastic cues of the conductor, who was elevated on his platform so all could see his gestures. The whole experience was amazing, but what really impacted me was the display of leadership I was observing. I pulled out my program bulletin and asked my friend for a pen. I began writing down every leadership lesson I was being exposed to right before my eyes.

My program bulletin was full of principles that I was filing away in the margins, between the sections, and anywhere I could find an empty space. I truly watched some of the greatest leadership in action during those two hours. My friends were ready to go when the concert concluded, but I was still writing down everything I wanted to incorporate into my leadership style. I didn't want it to be over. This even truly gave me a picture of how to orchestrate success while leading a team.

The lessons I wrote down that night are things I have come to live by, and now teach, over sixteen years later. Here is a picture of my program, which I still have:

The symphony is a fantastic and practical picture of how great leadership operates. A symphony orchestra concert has dynamic ebbs and flows of harmonious teamwork coming together to create an unforgettable experience. The team bands together to produce beautiful masterpieces of success throughout each piece of music. In the same way, people have the potential to create a masterpiece of success in their organization.

But it takes an extraordinary synergy of flow and dedication for that success to bond together into a symphony of leadership. Only when there are great players, playing great pieces, being lead by a great point person, playing at the right pace, will there be a concert of progress.

Traditional symphonies have what is called "four movements." These movements are the framework for a great concert. They create an unforgettable experience for the listener and the participants. I couldn't help but think that just as a symphony concert has four movements; four movements also create a great leadership culture. These four movements, or elements, are vital for an organization to operate at its optimal performance level. The whole flow of the symphony breaks down if just one of the movements is off.

Let's look at these four illustrative movements:

The First Movement
Choose The Right Players
You cannot have a great orchestra with mediocre players. The success of the sound depends on the quality of the musicians. As a musician myself, I know there is a big difference between someone who plays an instrument and someone who truly is a musician. Anyone can pick up an instrument and get a few notes from it, but it takes specialized skill to make the instrument produce beautiful sounds. For example, there are a whole lot of people who play guitar, but few who are truly guitar players. Too

many organizations settle for people who can pick a few notes instead of going after those who can produce greatness. The bar is set too low, allowing any player on the team. This may work in an all-inclusive band camp, but organizations that have a vital cause need the right people in place.

Many companies essentially let anyone who can pick up an instrument join their team, then wonder why amazing music isn't being produced. To become successful, there must be a high bar set for your team or you'll only attract average players. Not everyone can or needs to be part of your organization. I'm not sure if you got that last statement, so let me make it again...not everyone can or needs to be part of your organization.

> "You can have all the strategy, tools, and resources in the world, and still fall short if your people can't navigate them."

I have seen many organizations that never reach their potential because they simply had the wrong players playing. You can have all the strategy, tools, and resources in the world, and still fall short if your people can't navigate them. A team is only as good as its weakest link. Organizations that allow subpar players to join their team set themselves up for heartache and misery. It is very difficult, discouraging, and time consuming to continually have turnover in your organization by failing to get the right players. You can't allow desperation to lower your expectations. Desperation breeds depreciation. Depreciation causes you to undervalue what it takes and settle for whatever is available, which creates average work at best.

When you settle for average, you surrender your potential for greatness. Being so desperate for a body that you end up putting the wrong people in place can be the most detrimental of mistakes. People should be placed in roles based on strategy, not solely on necessity. Everyone loses when necessity overtakes strategy. The person who wasn't the right fit loses because they don't have what it takes to perform at the level needed of them. The people leading lose because they become increasingly frustrated with incompetence. And finally, the organization loses because it's not operating at its best. An organization is only at its best when the best people are playing in the ensemble.

You have to create high expectations on the front end if you want to get success on the back end. The good news is when you set the bar high; it filters out the wrong players and ends up elevating the right players. This is why elite teams are highly productive; the right players are in place. For example, The Navy SEALs send potential candidates through a strictly regimented tryout before they even consider a person an actual candidate for the SEALs. It is one of the hardest grueling military challenges in the world, with 75%-80% of candidates dropping out. And these dropouts are not average, run-of-the-mill, people; they are the top the Navy has to offer. Hell Week consists of five-and-a-half days of cold, wet, brutally difficult situations while operating on less than four hours of sleep. Only 25% even make it past Hell Week, which happens early on in the third week of phase one. That is staggering, considering the whole training is six months long, with a total of three phases.

The SEALs have the best of the best, and therefore are the best of the best. This is not happenstance or luck of the draw. They intentionally only allow the right players to even have a shot at playing. The fact that you make it to the top few who get selected for the SEALs is an amazing accomplishment within itself.

> "If you want to grow, don't hire for what you want to maintain; hire for where you want to go."

You may say, "Well sure—but that's the SEALs. Our organization isn't that regimented." This may be the case, but if you want to grow, don't hire for what you want to maintain; hire for where you want to go. The more you appreciate your organization and its mission, the more the players should appreciate in value. What you appreciate begins to appreciate in value. When you set the bar high, it will attract only those who play at a high level. The lower you set the bar, the more you'll attract low capacity players. If you want to be the best, you have to play with the best. You have to decide if you want to be an organization that settles, or an organization that is growing.

The Second Movement
Choose The Right Pieces

Not only do you need the right players, but you need to pick the right pieces for the players to play. Every great conductor capitalizes on the strengths of his or her team. Similarly, great athletic coaches know that as players leave and new ones come in, you must adjust your strategy based on the make-up of your new line up. Leaders must do likewise. Knowing who needs to play each part and allowing them to bring their unique skill to the piece allows for a masterpiece of success.

High-performance teams are fanatical about clearly defining expectations and executing them with precision. It is vital for the players to know exactly what to play and when to play it if they want to create a beautiful sound. Every individual musician in a symphony has clearly defined pieces to play at specific times. While I was at the concert observing this incredible group of musicians, I was mesmerized by their confidence in knowing the parts and the timing of when to come in. You could see the musicians begin to brace themselves for their upcoming cues.

Thus, when the conductor signaled, they could perform their part with excellence. Truly successful masterpieces do not just automatically happen. It was only through strategic practice and clarity that these musicians were confident enough to create harmony.

Every organization experiences the challenge of preserving clarity to ever increasing complexities. Players have to know the entire score inside and out. As an organization increases in opportunities, clarity naturally decreases in complexities. You have to fight to keep the main thing the main thing. Players have to focus on their specific contribution, or the whole piece can fall apart. Each person must be exceedingly responsible to play the right piece at the right time. Unlike athletics, a symphony relies upon every player to bring excellence to their part.

No one can carry the symphony all by themselves; not even the musicians with soloist parts. It's not that sports do not rely upon every player to do their part, but when others are not carrying their weight, at least a star athlete is able to rise up and carry the team in the short run. Symphonies do not have that luxury; they are completely dependent upon each person knowing their part. The clarinet player cannot play the percussion player's part if the percussionist falls behind. The tuba player cannot carry the cello player's part if she is not present. You will sabotage your potential if your organization is relying upon stars to carry the success of your team while others are allowed to operate under the radar. Every player on the team must be held accountable to progress and results.

> "You will sabotage your potential if your organization is relying upon stars to carry the success of your team while others are allowed to operate under the radar."

Economist Milton Friedman once said, "One of the great mistakes is to judge policies and programs by their intentions rather than their results." If someone is underperforming on the team, it will bring everything down. It's like the old boss who said, "Young man, I am going to give you a substantial raise."

The young man quickly responded, "When is it effective?"

"When you are!" the boss replied.

The reason people under produce is due to one of four components:

Lack Of Clarity

Because their leader's expectations are unclear, they do not know they are under producing. Sometimes all someone truly needs is more clearly defined metrics to achieve. For whatever reason, they are fuzzy on what is expected of them and what the target is they are shooting for. Vision blurs over time. It is imperative that expectations are over-communicated on a consistent basis.

Lack Of Competence

They do not know how to produce at a higher level and therefore need either training or termination. Many people just don't have what it takes to produce at a higher level. At this point, you have to decide if they need better training, or if they simply will never get better—even with training. If they are not able to respond to training, or have already received the training they need and are still under producing, they may need to be let go.

Lack Of Commitment

They do not want to produce and have lost the drive to move forward. Some people become burned out and have no gas left in the tank to keep moving forward. In such cases, you must determine if they need a break, need to be moved to another area that better fits them, or need to be released from the organization altogether. They will never perform at their best if they are not committed to the vision.

Lack Of Consequences

They are not held accountable for under producing and therefore suffer no consequences for their inactivity. Many people don't operate at their best because there are no repercussions for substandard performance if they don't. They naturally flow to the path of least resistance and end up cutting corners to do just enough to get by. There is nothing holding them accountable. Like a child always threatened but never disciplined for their unacceptable behavior, an underperforming team member will feel they can get away with anything.

When the right players are playing the right pieces, it's not hard to produce. You won't have to constantly look over everyone's shoulder and force them to get tasks done; they'll simply do it. Make sure your players know exactly what your expectations are and that they have everything they need to do well. Eliminate every excuse and you'll clearly know if the right players are able to play the right pieces.

Theodore Roosevelt said, "The best executive is the one who has sense enough to pick good men to do what he wants done, and self-restraint enough to keep from meddling with them while they do it."

The Third Movement

Choose The Right Point Person

As I sat in the audience of the symphony concert, I couldn't help but notice how important the conductor's role was. The conductor directs the symphony, and is thus the central person responsible to lead the musicians. The players watch the conductor's every move as they wait for direction. Clearly, the conductor is there to make sure everyone is playing their part in time and in tune. Every great symphony has a great conductor. In fact—the better the conductor, the better the symphony. The opposite is also true: the worse the conductor, the worse the symphony.

Even the best of players, playing the right pieces, can fall apart if the conductor is not the right fit. The conductor is the glue that holds the whole team together. Everyone needs someone to look up to and help guide them along their journey of success. Teams need coaches. A crew needs a captain. Soldiers need a commander. A child needs a parent or guardian. Symphonies need a conductor. Your employees or volunteers need a point person.

Far too many leaders fail to operate like a conductor. In fact, many leaders do the opposite of a conductor. They spend all of their time doing everyone else's job. They are caught in the doing and it keeps them from leading. This causes them to come down from their primary responsibility of directing the whole team. A leader must stay in their designated role as the conductor so they can give direction and oversight to the overall score of the team. The conductor I had the privilege of watching never came down from his platform to play the instruments for the players. After all, that would've weakened his ability to lead the whole team. What if the conductor spent his time doing all of the playing for the musicians? It would never let the players get better and learn their parts. A leader is responsible *to* their people, not *for* them. The moment you start feeling responsible for them is the moment you'll stop challenging and start coddling.

> "A leader is responsible *to* their people, not *for* them."

I also noticed the conductor was highly elevated so that all the musicians could see what to do and where to go. You can imagine if the conductor came down from his specific role, the team would have had no one to look to and to lead them. This shows how important it is for leaders to be visible to the team. They must be present, working with the team continuously, communicating, and directing. A conductor's primary function is to help the players come together and create a beautiful experience, just as a leader's job is to make sure the team is being equipped to do their part well. There would be no one to macro-lead the orchestra if a conductor spent all of his or her time micromanaging the players. The musicians have to learn to trust their conductor, just as the conductor has to trust the musicians. The conductor is there to get the best out of the musicians by practicing and performing with them. It is through this process that a symphony can learn to create beautiful music together.

I also saw that the conductor was highly enthusiastic. I have yet to see a great conductor who didn't bring passion and flare to their role. Conductors are known to be flamboyant figures, directing the players with intensity and gusto. I love watching these men and women conduct. They bring the music to life. It just makes you feel alive. In the same way, great leaders bring enthusiasm and passion to what they do. You will never see a highly successful person who is docile and melancholy. Ralph Waldo Emerson said, "Enthusiasm is one of the most powerful engines of success. When you do a thing, do it with all your might. Put your whole soul into it. Stamp it with your own personality. Be active, be energetic, be enthusiastic and faithful, and you will accomplish your object. Nothing great was ever achieved without enthusiasm."

If you observe anyone who is highly successful at what they do, you'll notice they all bring a strong passion to their craft. There is an energy that exudes from them when they perform. This is because they are in their sweet spot, making things happen, and it lights them up. Having the right point person to lead a team makes all of the difference in the team's performance and morale. Only put people at the conductor level who exude a high level of passion and enthusiasm for what they do. Nothing kills a team's performance more than a disinterested and disengaged leader who seems lifeless.

The Fourth Movement

Choose The Right Pace

To bring about emotion and feeling, the symphony orchestra plays everything in a precise time signature. The timing of the music determines the feeling of the emotion. Even when you have the right players, playing the right pieces, with the right point person, all must still be playing at the right pace and in sync with one another.

Music has rhythm, and success has a rhythm as well. There is a groove to success that must be played. Playing too fast or too slow can change the whole rhythm of a song. During my own musical journey, it took me a while to figure out how to play in time with a metronome. The funny thing about that tick-tock of a metronome is that it never changes—but boy, does a person's timing change. I heard a struggling musician once say, "I've yet to find a metronome that doesn't speed up or slow down." Of course, the issue wasn't the metronome, but the musician himself, weaving in and out of the time signature.

Success is like a metronome; there is a disciplined pace that one must take to ensure a masterpiece. In my experience with musicians, almost all tend to speed up while trying to stay in time. Rarely do people slow down for some reason. I guess it is in our nature to want to speed up. It's probably our fast-paced, fast food, microwave culture that tries to rush everything. But success is not a short, open sprint; it's a marathon with hurdles and obstacles. Organizations that set themselves up for the long haul are the ones who experience not just success, but significance as well.

> "Execute as if there's no tomorrow, but plan as if you'll live forever."

Significance is about leaving a legacy. It's about creating a lasting endeavor that stands the test of time. Short-sighted leadership creates fleeting fads. A leader's eyes must be on the future. I had a mentor that used to tell me, "Always be thinking down the road, because you'll be there sooner than you think." Execute as if there's no tomorrow, but plan as if you'll live forever.

Every great leader knows that if you want to have a sustainable level of success, you have to practice patience. It will always take longer than you thought and be harder than you anticipated. President Franklin D. Roosevelt understood the importance of keeping a country together while moving forward. Faced with one of the greatest economic crises in American history, FDR led the people through the Great Depression amidst World War II. He once stated, "A good leader can't get too far ahead of his followers." President Roosevelt kept a healthy pace allowing him to lead the country without losing sight of the people in the process.

Without the discipline of patience, you will give up and bail out from your pursuit of success. The journey of a successful enterprise must be built on patience. Thinking you will be an overnight success is not reality. In fact, I once heard it said that anyone can become an overnight success after 20 years of hard work. The journey to success is the daily process of pressing on even when it gets tough. Patience is the name of the game.

But you can't truly have patience unless you couple it with endurance. Endurance is the ability to have patience, and patience is the ability to endure. So, to experience significance as an effective leader, you must extract endurance within yourself and your team. You have to reach deep within and labor from a place of purpose and dedication to your cause. If you don't have an unwavering sense of determination, you will give up when things get shaky...and things always get shaky. Radio personality Paul Harvey used to say, "You can tell you're on the road to success; it's uphill all the way." The more patience a leader possesses, the more success they'll experience in the long run.

Get the right players, playing the right pieces, being directed by the right point person, playing at the same pace, and you will begin to come into harmony with lasting significance in all you do.

Questions To Think About:

A) Articulate how an organization is like a giant symphony?

_____

_____

_____

B) Circle which of the 4 movements are the most challenging for you and explain why?

The Right Players   **The Right Pieces**

The Right Point Person   **The Right Pace**

_____

_____

_____

C) How will your organization leave a significant legacy?

_____

_____

_____

Leadology Challenge:

Is your organization operating like a well-rehearsed symphony orchestra? If so, what is letting it function so well? You need to study your success as much as your failures. If we don't know why we are successful, how can we fix it if things ever go wrong?

If your organization is not functioning well, which of the four movements are struggling the most? Identify the areas that are not playing in unison with the vision. If just one of the pieces, the players, the point person, or the pace is off, it will sabotage the whole score. Master conductors can quickly identify what is wrong with the orchestra. They see and hear from a high level vantage point, allowing them to decipher what needs to be fixed. You too must ensure that you are leading in a way that keeps the whole entirety of the symphony together. Listen carefully, watch observantly, lead enthusiastically, and communicate candidly. Pinpoint the areas that are off and make the necessary corrections to keep the flow of the movements progressing forward.

|| Conclusion ||

Thank you so much for reading *Leadology* and expanding your cognitive leadership library. Remember what Oliver Wendell Holmes said: "One's mind, once stretched by a new idea, never regains its original dimensions." Now is time to take what you've learned through this book by applying the ideas, strategies, and challenges to level up your leadership. Never stop consuming resources that will multiply your ability to lead effectively.

The more you know, the more you grow. And the more you grow, the more you'll know. Wise leaders take their knowledge and put it to use. They oscillate from knowledge to action; and then from action to knowledge. In other words, they learn then act, and then learn from their actions. This is how they continue to level up again and again increasing their ideas, influence, impact, and income.

I hope this book helped you in your leadership journey. If there is anyone you know that would benefit from this resource, please let them know about it so you can help them level up as well.

I would love the honor to come alongside and help guide you and your team to the next level. Please check out my website at www.johnbarrettleadership.com for more resources and to find the ways we could partner together to help you win.

About The Author...

John is a sought after leadership coach, speaker, and trainer. He has been living and teaching leadership for over sixteen years. John has been personally mentored by world renown leadership expert, Dr. John C. Maxwell, and a host of other highly successful leaders. He has coached Fortune 5,000 companies, entrepreneurs, non-profits, and individuals who desire to level up their success.

John has been interviewed on radio programs, podcasts, blogs, and many other platforms, reaching over 200,000 listeners. He is dedicated to guiding others to the next level on their leadership journey.

Bulk Discount Pricing

When you help your team develop their leadership ability, your organization will experience greater success as a result. Provide a copy of Leadology for each person on your team and see what opportunities begin to open up. Contact us at www.johnbarrettleadership.com to purchase.

Visit John's website to find out more info…

✓ About

✓ Leadership Coaching

✓ Business Coaching

✓ Life Coaching

✓ Speaking

✓ Leadership Art

✓ Books

✓ Blog

www.JohnBarrettLeadership.com

Book John To Speak At Your Event

Notes…

Notes…

www.ingramcontent.com/pod-product-compliance
Lightning Source LLC
Chambersburg PA
CBHW021358090426
42742CB00009B/903